ALSO BY PAT AND GINA NEELY

Down Home with the Neelys

The Neelys' Celebration Cookbook

BACK HOME *with* THE NEELYS

BACK HOME *with* THE NEELYS

Comfort Food from
Our Southern Kitchen to Yours

Pat and Gina Neely

with Ann Volkwein

Photographs by Alex Farnum

 ALFRED A. KNOPF | NEW YORK | 2014

THIS IS A BORZOI BOOK
PUBLISHED BY ALFRED A. KNOPF

www.aaknopf.com

Knopf, Borzoi Books, and the colophon are
registered trademarks of Random House LLC.

Library of Congress Cataloging-in-Publication Data
Neely, Patrick.
Back home with the Neelys / by Patrick Neely and Gina Neely; with
Ann Volkwein; photographs by Alex Farnum. —First Edition.
pages cm
Includes index.
ISBN 978-0-307-96133-4
ISBN 978-0-307-96134-1 (eBook)
1. Cooking, American–Southern style. I. Neely, Gina. II. Title.
TX715.2.S68N433 2014
641.5975—dc20
2013047419

Jacket photograph © Alex Farnum
Jacket design by Kelly Blair

Manufactured in the United States of America
First Edition

Dedication

Writing this book brought back so many fond memories from my childhood growing up in the South. My ancestors who grew their own vegetables and raised their animals were true pioneers from a culinary standpoint.

   I dedicate this book to all the men and women from several generations ago who inspired and encouraged—and introduced me to the culinary arts!

Pat

To all families who embrace, support, and believe in passing on time-tested traditions . . . let's bring them all back, and quick. Enjoy!

Gina

Contents

Introduction ix

Jams, Preserves, Breads, and Biscuits 3

Breakfast 21

Appetizers, Snacks, and Small Bites 33

Side Dishes, Veggies, and Salads 55

Meats 89

Smoked and Grilled 115

Sandwiches 137

Casseroles, Soups, and Stews 151

Sweets 171

Gina's Southern Cocktails 191

Acknowledgments 203

Index 205

Introduction

People often ask us about our culinary roots and when we first recognized our love for food and cooking. We never have a quick answer to that question. If you are born and raised in the South, your entire life revolves around Southern food. Southern techniques and attitudes become deeply embedded in your cooking styles, and that has certainly been true for us. But the question always gets us thinking about the family and friends that first fed us and taught us. Their recipes have come to occupy a place in our personal history and present-day meal making, and in this book we've gathered many of them, as well as a handful of stories. You want to find out about someone? Have him cook a meal for you.

We have long had an appreciation for down-home cooking and fresh ingredients, and it all goes back to the wonderful memories we have of growing up in Memphis. Those were the good old days, when everything was fresh and plentiful. Even after our grandparents moved from "the Country" to the city, farmers still came through the neighborhood in their open-bed trucks with fresh produce. Our grandparents used their backyards as gardens, and most of the vegetables our parents and grandparents cooked with were grown in them. We don't think they knew what organic food was, but talk about organic! As kids, we felt there was nothing better than stepping outside and picking what was ripe that day. We didn't appreciate how blessed we were to have this as part of our childhood. Local ingredients define our regional cooking. Of course, it's what you do with those ingredients that counts. Once we get in the kitchen, we always put our spin on them—not too much, just enough to suit our current tastes without losing out on the big flavor payoffs that these ingredients in familiar recipes are known to deliver.

From Small Batch Strawberry Jam to Deep-Fried Pickles, Blackened Catfish with Creole Rémoulade to Stewed Pinto Beans, Sausage Cream Gravy and Biscuits to Mama Daisy's Chocolate-Frosted Cake, ours has been a true Southern journey. The recipes we have chosen to share with you in this book mean a lot to us, and we hope they bring as much joy to you and your family as they have to ours!

Pat and Gina

BACK HOME *with* THE NEELYS

Jams, Preserves, Breads, and Biscuits

Small Batch Strawberry Jam

Hot Pepper Jelly

Pickled Peppers

Sweet Pickled Relish

Pickled Okra

Compound Butters: Cinnamon Honey Butter and Herb Butter

Easy Buttermilk and Cream Biscuits

Old-Fashioned Yeast Rolls

Green Onion and Cheddar Quick Bread

Skillet Corn Bread

Gina I believe that when you're cooking with great ingredients, the simplest recipes are always best. This is certainly true of our Small Batch Strawberry Jam, which uses just strawberries, sugar, and lemon juice. The fresher the strawberries, the better the jam. Whenever I make it, I think back to how much fun I used to have picking strawberries from Nana's garden, and how excited everyone was when I'd return to the house with a pail-full of juicy fruit. I loved watching Nana turn my pickings into delicious jam, and it tasted even better with some of her yeast rolls (they were nothing short of legendary!). Remembering the process inspired me to try my own jammin' and preservin', and I borrowed recipes from Nana, Mama Callie, and Mama Daisy to share with you. Now go pick some strawberries and get started!

Small Batch Strawberry Jam

Gina This version of jammin' is a simple process that uses just three ingredients. All you need are sunshine-fresh strawberries, sugar, and lemon juice. Then just allow the natural flavors to step in and do their work. People often don't realize how easy it is to make jam. This recipe is always eaten quickly in our house and tastes great spread on hot Sunday morning buttery biscuits, in sandwiches, or even as a topping for vanilla ice cream. I like to toast some thick brioche and pile the strawberry jam on top for a sweet dessert to end my day.

---

1 pound fresh strawberries, hulled and roughly chopped

1 cup plus 1 tablespoon sugar

Juice of 1 lemon

Heat an 8-ounce Mason jar and lid in simmering water (see Canning Method, page 7, for detailed instructions).

Put the strawberries, sugar, and lemon juice in a large bowl, and toss well together. Let stand for 5 minutes, so their natural juices begin to develop. Pour the mixture into a saucepan, and, over medium heat, bring to a boil. Continue to cook, stirring, until jam is thick, about 10 minutes.

Carefully ladle jam into the clean Mason jar. Wipe the rim clean, and let cool to room temperature. Cover jar, and store in refrigerator for up to 10 days.

Makes about 1 cup

Tip If you want to process the jam fully, for longer storage, follow the instructions in the Canning Method (see page 7).

Hot Pepper Jelly

Gina Hot-pepper jelly reminds me of all the time I spent in the parlor as a young girl. You know, the room off to the side of the house with a sofa, side table, lamp, candle, and beautiful flower arrangement. I used to invite my friends over for some old-school entertaining in the parlor, just like I had seen my mom do. We'd get out the sweet tea (the house wine of the South), grab the homemade hot-pepper jelly and sourdough bread, and gossip for hours.

You can spread this pepper jelly over chicken or any other meat as a glaze, spoon it over a brick of cream cheese or Brie and serve it with crackers, or use it in a club sandwich. Or, honey, get that Mason jar, wrap a ribbon around it, and give it as a gift that's sure to bring a smile to someone's face or warm their heart. That's true old-school entertaining—that's how I remember this pepper jelly.

---

2 medium red bell peppers, seeded and roughly chopped

1 medium orange bell pepper, seeded and roughly chopped

9 medium jalapeños, roughly chopped

1¼ cups white vinegar

One 1.75-ounce box Sure-Jell fruit pectin

1 tablespoon unsalted butter

5 cups sugar

1 teaspoon kosher salt

Heat four 12-ounce Mason jars and lids in simmering water (see Canning Method, opposite, for detailed instructions).

Working in three batches, add the peppers and jalapeños to the bowl of a food processor, and pulse together fifteen times. Do not purée until completely smooth; we're looking for a slightly chunky texture.

Transfer the mixture from the food processor to a large Dutch oven (or any large, heavy-bottomed pot). Over medium heat, stir in the vinegar, pectin, and butter. Keep stirring, and bring the mixture to a strong rolling boil. Once it's boiling, stir in the sugar and salt, and continue stirring until the mixture comes back up to a rolling boil. Cook and stir for another full minute. Remove from the heat, and carefully skim the top of the jelly for any foam.

See Canning Method (opposite) for remaining instructions. If you do not want to process or can the jelly, it will also keep stored in the refrigerator for 1 month.

Makes four 12-ounce jars

Tip If you are not too keen on red, yellow, or green bell peppers, you can use fruit as well. Blackberries, raspberries, and figs taste great.

CANNING

Gina Canning was a necessity, not a luxury, to our grandparents. Canning everything from their garden when it was ripe gave them a nutritious way to sustain themselves through the winter. (And when there was a bumper crop, it meant nothing ever went to waste!) But canning also allowed the ingredients to marinate and their flavors to intensify over time, adding to the deep flavors so inherent in Southern cooking.

CANNING METHOD

Start by sterilizing your jars and lids. First hand-wash the jars in hot soapy water, or run them through a cycle in your dishwasher. Now, to protect the jars from touching the bottom of the pot and overheating, place a rack on the bottom of a deep pot or a canner (if you're using a canner, it should come with a rack). Place the jars, open side up, on the rack; then fill the pot with water, making sure the jars are also filled with water. The water should cover the jars by a few inches. Cover the pot, bring to a simmer, and heat jars for 10 minutes. This not only sterilizes the jars but also prevents the glass from breaking later on, during processing. Turn off the heat, and leave the jars in the hot water while you prepare the recipe. Add the lids to a separate, smaller saucepan, cover with water, bring to a simmer, and remove from heat. Let the lids sit in the hot water while you prepare the jelly.

When the jelly is ready, remove the jars and lids from the hot water with tongs. Place the jars on a clean kitchen towel to dry, and carefully hand-dry the lids. Once they're dry, carefully hold each jar with a kitchen towel, place a wide-mouth funnel at the top of the jar, and ladle in the jam, leaving about ¼ inch of room at the top. Wipe the rims clean, and firmly tighten the sterilized lids.

Carefully submerge the jars in the pot with the hot water again, and bring to a boil. Cover with a lid, and gently boil for 10 minutes. Let the jars cool for a few minutes before removing them from the pot, then place them on your kitchen counter to cool to room temperature. Check the jars after 12 hours to make sure they have sealed. The tops should have popped in. To test this, push the center of each lid. If the lid does not pop up and down when pressed, the jars are sealed.

Refrigerate any jar that did not seal, and eat that batch first, within a month of making the jelly. Store sealed jams in a cool, dark place up to a year. Once they've been opened, they will keep up to a month in the refrigerator.

Pickled Peppers

Pat I love my food spicy, but my girls always complain that I make everything too hot. If your home is like mine, then you need to pickle some of your own peppers. I learned this from my grandfather, who used to keep a jar of peppers on the table. Whether he was adding a few peppers to my grandmother's turnip greens, or pouring some of the juice on her meatloaf, he always added a little kick to whatever she served for dinner. Now, forty years later, I find myself doing the same thing!

1 pound mixed hot peppers (red and green jalapeños, serranos, and banana peppers)

4 cups white vinegar

2 cups water

3 tablespoons kosher salt

2 tablespoons granulated white sugar

1 tablespoon brown sugar

3 cloves garlic

2 dried bay leaves

2 sprigs fresh thyme

1 teaspoon whole black peppercorns

Heat two 1-quart Mason jars and lids in simmering water (see Canning Method, page 7, for detailed instructions). Prick each whole pepper with a paring knife, and pack the peppers into both jars.

Put the vinegar, water, salt, sugars, garlic, bay leaves, thyme sprigs, and black peppercorns in a medium-sized saucepan, and bring to a boil. Reduce the heat, and simmer for 5 minutes. This will help to marry the flavors and to dissolve the salt and sugar.

Carefully top each jar with the simmering vinegar mixture, leaving about ¼ inch of room at the top. Push gently on the peppers to make sure they fill with the pickling liquid. Wipe the rims clean, and firmly tighten the lids on the jars. If canning, follow the Canning Method instructions on page 7. Wait 3 days before eating. Once open, store in the refrigerator for up to a week.

Makes two 1-quart jars

Sweet Pickled Relish

Gina Everyone in the South is familiar with sweet pickled relish (if you're not, I need to speak with you alone), and it has become a faithful companion to any barbecue dish. My sister Tanya loved pickles so much she used to soak cucumbers in a bowl of vinegar and eat them straight out of the fridge. Now, I'm not suggesting you try that, but I do bet that once you try this recipe you won't be buying relish in the supermarket anymore. This recipe is just as sweet, and the sugar offsets the vinegar to make it truly delicious.

5 cups finely diced pickling cucumbers
(about 6 cucumbers)
1½ cups finely diced Vidalia onion
(about ½ large onion)
1 cup finely chopped red bell pepper
(about 1 small pepper)

2 tablespoons kosher salt
1 cup white vinegar
½ cup sugar
1 teaspoon celery seeds
1 teaspoon mustard seeds

Put the vegetables in a large colander set in the sink. Sprinkle with the salt, and let sit and drain for 2 hours. After 2 hours, rinse the vegetables under cold water and shake dry. Squeeze the excess water from them with a clean kitchen towel.

Put the vinegar, sugar, celery seeds, and mustard seeds in a large saucepan, and bring to a boil. Reduce heat, and simmer for 3 minutes. Add the veggies and return to a boil, stirring on occasion. Boil for 8 minutes, stirring occasionally. Then remove from heat. When it has cooled completely, ladle into clean jars. This will keep refrigerated up to 1 month.

Makes about 3 cups

Tip If you want to process the relish, follow the instructions in the Canning Method on page 7, but process for 15 minutes rather than 10. We don't bother to do this, though, because this stuff goes way too fast in our family.

Pickled Okra

Pat Okra is classic Southern veggie that's finally becoming more popular at farmers' markets and restaurants. Mama Rena (my granny) grew okra in her backyard garden, and it was usually a part of one of her weekday meals. I used to love okra fried, but Gina didn't acquire a taste for the vegetable until she had it pickled. She says it was then that she decided her palate must be "maturing." Black peppercorns, red-pepper flakes, and caraway seeds give this okra just the right amount of kick, and it works well as a garnish in a Southern-style martini or Bloody Mary (or simply eaten alone at cocktail time).

1½ cups apple-cider vinegar

½ cup water

2 tablespoons kosher salt

1 tablespoon sugar

¾ teaspoon mustard seeds

¼ teaspoon whole black peppercorns

¼ teaspoon red-pepper flakes

¼ teaspoon caraway seeds

12 ounces small fresh okra

Hand-wash four pint jars in hot soapy water, or run through a cycle in your dishwasher. Heat the jars and their lids in simmering water (see Canning Method, page 7, for detailed instructions).

Heat the vinegar, water, salt, sugar, mustard seeds, peppercorns, pepper flakes, and caraway seeds in a medium saucepan until boiling. Reduce heat, and simmer for 5 minutes, stirring to dissolve the salt and sugar.

Pack your jars with okra, and top with the simmering vinegar mixture, leaving ¼ inch of room at the top. Cover with lid, and cool to room temperature. Store in the refrigerator, and start sampling in 10 days.

Makes 1 quart

Tip If you want to process the okra, follow the instructions in the Canning Method on page 7, but process for 15 minutes instead of 10.

Tip If you choose not to do the full Canning Method, these will keep in the refrigerator for about 1 month.

Compound Butters

Gina Compound butters are easy to fix, and they make a big statement on the table. You basically just smash softened butter with a rubber spatula and add any herb or spice that floats your boat, sweet or savory. They're my secret weapon for entertaining, because they last for two weeks in the refrigerator and up to two months in the freezer, so it's easy to always have some on hand for unexpected guests. The cinnamon honey butter is great for brunches and goes well with biscuits, muffins, and toast. Add herb butter made with chives to complete a simple dish of mashed potatoes, or, Pat's favorite, two dollops of herb butter to a backyard-grilled rib-eye steak. Now we're talkin'!

Cinnamon Honey Butter

1 stick (½ cup) salted butter, softened
1 tablespoon honey

¼ teaspoon ground cinnamon

Put the softened butter in a small bowl. Drizzle in the honey and add the cinnamon, and thoroughly combine with a rubber spatula. Lay out a large sheet of plastic wrap on your work surface, and spread out the butter along the center. Roll up the butter in the plastic wrap, and form into a log shape about 12 inches long. Twist the ends of the plastic wrap to seal. Set in the freezer until chilled and hard. Slice into rounds to top Easy Buttermilk and Cream Biscuits (page 15) or our Skillet Corn Bread (page 18).

Herb Butter

1 stick (½ cup) salted butter, softened
2 tablespoons chopped mixed fresh
   herbs (such as parsley, basil, chives)

1 clove garlic, minced
Freshly ground black pepper

Put the softened butter in a small bowl. Sprinkle in the herbs, garlic, and pepper, and thoroughly combine with a rubber spatula. Lay out a large sheet of plastic wrap on your work surface, and spread out the butter along the center. Roll up the butter in the plastic wrap, and form into a log shape. Twist the ends of the plastic wrap to seal. Set in the freezer until chilled and hard. Slice into rounds to top biscuits or bread.

MAMA DAISY (Daisy Carter)

Pat I truly believe that if Mama Daisy, my maternal grandmother, was alive today, she would be a pastry chef. This woman could really bake—cookies, triple-layer cakes, pies, brownies—and her corn bread was amazing.

Mama Daisy was a big fan of routine. She rose early every morning to clean the house. (I often thought she would buff the paint right off the furniture!) She'd then start preparing lunch for my grandfather. He was a lucky man to come home for lunch and find Mama Daisy's food waiting for him every day. On Friday afternoons, Mama Daisy used to wait for my grandfather to come home so they could go to the grocery store together. They had only one car, and I don't believe she ever learned how to drive. I loved spending time at their house on Fridays, because after she finished putting the groceries away, she always made her famous hamburgers with homemade fries. And after dinner, there was always something under the domed cake plate for dessert. My favorite was Mama Daisy's Chocolate-Frosted Cake (page 175).

Easy Buttermilk and Cream Biscuits

Pat Mama Daisy was known around the neighborhood as the "Biscuit Queen." She made biscuits every Sunday morning, so as a kid I couldn't wait to visit our grandparents on the weekends. She and my grandfather were early risers and would start cooking around 6 a.m. Everyone had to be at the breakfast table by 8 a.m. My grandfather was usually in the back-yard feeding his dogs, and there were two things that were always exciting to wake up to: the amazing smell of fresh breakfast coming from her tiny kitchen, and the sound of her call from the back porch, signaling to my grandfather that breakfast was ready.

I always wished Mama Daisy had written down her recipes, but she didn't. She cooked every day, and her recipes became so routine she was able to cook completely from memory. We tried to duplicate this recipe based purely on my memories, and I think we came pretty close.

---

2 cups all-purpose flour, plus more
  for dusting
1 tablespoon baking powder
1 tablespoon sugar

1½ teaspoons kosher salt
1 cup heavy cream
½ cup low-fat buttermilk
1 tablespoon salted butter, melted

Preheat the oven to 425 degrees F.

In a medium bowl, whisk together the flour, baking powder, sugar, and salt. Stir in cream and buttermilk until the dough just comes together, being careful not to overwork the dough.

Dust your countertop with flour, and dump the dough on top. Knead for about 1 minute, or until the dough looks smooth. Pat the dough out to a ¾-inch thickness. Punch out the biscuits with a 2-inch biscuit cutter. Rework the dough scraps, and cut rounds out of the remaining dough.

Place the biscuits on a baking tray, brush with melted butter, and bake for 20 minutes, until puffed and golden brown.

Makes 12 biscuits

Old-Fashioned Yeast Rolls

Gina Nana used to reserve her yeast rolls for holidays, church functions, and special occasions, but we all loved them so much they soon became a regular feature on the dinner table. It got to the point where dinner didn't seem complete without them. She would make big batches to share with everyone in the neighborhood, and I remember how special it felt when she gave some to me and Pat. I still crave these rolls, and my girls have fallen in love with them, too. They're soft and luscious and easy to make. Sometimes it's the small things that have the biggest impact to create a great meal.

¼ cup warm water (105 to 115 degrees F)

One ¼-ounce package active dry yeast

2 tablespoons plus 2 teaspoons sugar, divided

3½ cups all-purpose flour, plus more for dusting

2½ teaspoons kosher salt, plus more for sprinkling

½ cup whole milk

½ cup sour cream

4 tablespoons unsalted butter, melted and cooled

Nonstick spray

1 large egg, slightly beaten

Put water, yeast, and 1 teaspoon sugar in a small bowl, and mix together. Let stand for 5 minutes, until foamy like a frothy beer.

Add flour, remaining sugar, and salt to the bowl of a stand mixer fitted with a dough hook. Run the mixer on low until the ingredients are combined. In a separate bowl, combine milk, sour cream, and melted butter, and whisk until smooth.

While the mixer is running on low, slowly pour in the foamy yeast mixture, then the milk mixture, and let the mixer run for 2 minutes. Then increase the speed to medium and run for an additional 4 minutes. The dough should look smooth and elastic.

Spray a large bowl with nonstick spray. Add dough, and flip to coat with oil. Cover with a clean tea towel, and let rest for 1½ hours.

Lightly dust your work surface with some flour. Turn out the dough, and knead just a few times. Cut your dough into eighteen equal-sized pieces. Roll each piece into a ball until smooth and round. Place on a parchment-lined sheet tray, and cover with a tea towel. Let rest again, for 1¼ hours.

Preheat your oven to 375 degrees F.

Whisk together the egg and 1 tablespoon water in a small bowl. Brush each roll with the egg wash, and sprinkle tops lightly with salt. Bake until golden, 15 to 18 minutes.

Makes 18 rolls

Green Onion and Cheddar Quick Bread

Pat This is not the first bread we've developed using cheddar (*Down Home with the Neelys* features a broccoli and cheddar corn bread), but wait until you taste the classic Southern combination of green onions and cheddar. If you're working with a partner in the kitchen, do as we do: one person handles the wet ingredients and the other the dry. This bread is a hearty accompaniment for chili or stews, and great served toasted with a fried egg for breakfast. Just remember to be patient, and let the bread cool completely before slicing. If you slice it too soon, it will be gummy and undercooked around the bottom edges.

Nonstick spray
2¾ cups all-purpose flour
2 tablespoons sugar
1 tablespoon baking powder
2 teaspoons mustard powder
2 teaspoons kosher salt
¼ teaspoon baking soda
¼ teaspoon granulated garlic

1 cup finely diced yellow cheddar cheese (4 ounces)
3 green onions, chopped
1½ cups buttermilk
4 tablespoons salted butter, melted and cooled
1 large egg

Preheat oven to 350 degrees F. Spray a 9-by-5-inch loaf pan with nonstick spray. In a large bowl, whisk together the flour, sugar, baking powder, mustard powder, salt, baking soda, and garlic. Once they're mixed, add the cheese and green onions. Use your hands to toss the ingredients, and make sure all the cheese is coated with flour. In a separate bowl, whisk together the buttermilk, butter, and egg. Add the wet ingredients to the dry, and stir together until just combined. Spoon the batter (it will be thick and heavy) into the prepared loaf pan. Smooth out the top of the batter so it's even. Bake for 50 to 55 minutes, or until a toothpick inserted in the center comes out clean. Cool in the pan for 10 minutes, then turn out onto a wire rack. Let cool completely before slicing.

Makes one 9-by-5-inch loaf

BREADBOXES

Mama Daisy always had a breadbox on her counter. If you haven't seen one, it's a simple wooden or metal case with a door on it to preserve bread, cookies, and biscuits. In those days, breadboxes were necessary, because all our bread was baked fresh, without any of the preservatives that you find in the plastic-wrapped, sliced bread you can buy off the shelf in the grocery stores. Fresh bread keeps much longer at room temperature than it does in the refrigerator. The lid lets in just enough air to prevent mold, but is tight enough to protect the bread. As artisanal bread baking has caught on in recent years, I've been pleased to see classic breadboxes making a comeback.

Skillet Corn Bread

Gina Skillet corn bread has always been my go-to comfort food, and my mom used to make it for me as a treat when I was younger. I do this for my girls now whenever I think they need a little love. The trick to really good corn bread is preheating the skillet, then baking the corn bread right in the hot skillet, so you build a crispy crust. This recipe is our version of the classic hot-water corn bread we grew up on, which was made by mixing cornmeal with hot water until it felt like mashed potatoes, then frying it in a skillet with oil and bacon grease. Most Southern corn bread recipes tend to be a bit sweet, and I like to top mine off with a little of our Cinnamon Honey Butter (page 12).

2¼ cups ground yellow cornmeal
1¾ cups all-purpose flour
2 tablespoons sugar
2 teaspoons baking powder
2¼ teaspoons kosher salt

1¾ cups buttermilk
One 8¼-ounce can creamed corn
2 large eggs, beaten
5 tablespoons unsalted butter, melted, divided

Preheat oven to 375 degrees F. Place a 10-inch cast-iron skillet on the center rack while it heats.

Whisk together the cornmeal, flour, sugar, baking powder, and salt in a medium bowl. In a separate bowl, whisk together the buttermilk, creamed corn, eggs, and 3 tablespoons of the melted butter. Stir the wet ingredients into the dry until just combined.

Carefully remove the hot skillet from the oven, and add the remaining 2 tablespoons of melted butter, swirling to make sure it reaches all the edges of the skillet. Pour in the batter, and spread evenly across the pan. Bake for 30 minutes. Best when served fresh and warm.

Serves 8 to 10

SEASONING A CAST-IRON SKILLET

Gina I remember asking my grandmother about the long seasoning process she went through every time she purchased what I thought were the heaviest skillets in the world. She used to tell me we had to "cook the flavor" into the skillet. Her method was to take traditional shortening and rub it all over the skillet, inside and out. Then she'd place it upside down in a 350-degree-F oven and let it cook for an hour. As I started spending more time in the kitchen, I grew up to appreciate the flavor cast-iron skillets lent to the food cooked in them (and be able to lift them). Just remember, when you're cleaning cast iron, never use soap or you'll have to reseason it! While the pan is still warm, run it under hot water and use a soft scrub brush.

Breakfast

Eggs and Cheese Grits

Pecan Flapjacks

Bourbon French Toast

Breakfast Pot Pie

Griddled and Glazed Ham and Eggs

Sausage Cream Gravy and Biscuits

Gina When I was growing up, my mom and grandmother would not allow us to leave the house without eating breakfast. They always said, "You can't learn anything on an empty stomach." To this day, it feels wrong when I don't eat breakfast, and it's become one of my favorite meals to make for my girls. We take our breakfast seriously in the South, and Pat and I have collected the best of our family's good ole-fashion breakfast grub to share with you. From grits to Sausage Cream Gravy, griddled ham, and a Breakfast Pot Pie, these recipes will start the day off right.

Eggs and Cheese Grits

Gina Grits are a staple on the Southern breakfast table, and there are a lot of different ways to prepare them. We like ours with a little cheese (okay, a lot of cheese), so I refer to this dish as "grits with a twist." You'll start the grits, then make the eggs in a separate pan while the eggs cook. We add mozzarella to the eggs, which melts really well and keeps them moist. Make sure to cook the eggs slowly, over low heat. When they're done, scoop them on top of the grits, and add green onion for color.

GRITS	EGGS
2 cups homemade or low-sodium chicken stock or water	12 large eggs
2 cups whole milk	2 tablespoons heavy cream
Pinch of sugar	Kosher salt and freshly ground black pepper
Kosher salt and freshly ground black pepper	2 tablespoons salted butter
1 cup quick-cooking grits	¾ cup shredded mozzarella cheese
2 ounces cream cheese, sliced into cubes	2 green onions, thinly sliced, plus more for garnish

Put the stock or water, milk, sugar, and a big pinch of salt in a large saucepan, and bring to a boil.

Once it's boiling, add the grits gradually, in a slow, steady stream, whisking constantly. Reduce the heat to low, and stir frequently until the liquid is absorbed and the grits become thick, about 10 minutes. Stir in the cream cheese, taste, and adjust seasoning as needed. (Sometimes grits need a lot of salt.)

Meanwhile, crack the eggs into a large bowl, add the heavy cream, and whisk until smooth. Season with salt and pepper. Heat a large nonstick skillet over medium heat, and add the butter. Once it is melted and foamy, stir in the eggs. Stir the eggs continually with a rubber spatula until creamy curds form, about 4 to 5 minutes. Sprinkle in the cheese and the green onions, and fold the eggs over themselves to soften the cheese. Remove from heat.

Plate the grits in a bowl, and top with eggs. Sprinkle with some more green onions for a pop of color.

Serves 4

Pecan Flapjacks

Pat There is nothing, I mean nothing, like a good ole Southern morning. Whether you call these flapjacks, pancakes, or hotcakes, it doesn't really matter. My mom and grandmother would always start cooking early in the morning, before any of us were awake. But they never got too far along. We could smell the aroma coming from the kitchen and hear the sizzle from the skillet, so we were always waiting with empty plates by the time they were finished. They had a way of adding something a little special to their flapjacks, like fresh blueberries or strawberries, but all Gina and I could think about when we started making these were pecans.

When we make these together, I mix the dry ingredients and Gina mixes the wet. Then I create a well in the center of my dry ingredients so that Gina can pour in her mixture and easily incorporate all the ingredients. Your griddle must be hot, and the nonstick spray makes it easy to flip these jacks. You'll know when it's time to flip because small bubbles will appear on the outer circle of your jacks and start to burst.

2 cups unbleached all-purpose flour
¼ cup sugar
½ teaspoon kosher salt
1 tablespoon baking powder
2 cups whole milk
2 large eggs

¼ cup unsalted butter, melted and cooled, plus another 2 tablespoons for cooking
Nonstick spray
1 cup chopped pecans
Warm maple syrup, for serving

In a large bowl, whisk together flour, sugar, salt, and baking powder.

In a medium bowl, whisk together the milk, eggs, and melted butter until blended. Make a well in the center of the dry ingredients, and add the wet. Stir to combine until just mixed; some small lumps are good.

Heat a large griddle over medium heat. Spray lightly with nonstick spray, and brush lightly with melted butter. Use a ¼-cup dry measure or ladle to scoop the batter onto the griddle. Sprinkle each cake evenly with 1 scant tablespoon of chopped pecans. Cook the flapjacks on the first side for 1½ to 2 minutes, or until small bubbles begin to burst around the edges. Flip the cake, and cook the other side for 2 minutes. Serve with warm maple syrup.

Serves 4

Bourbon French Toast

Pat I love French toast. And, oh, by the way, I love bourbon as well. This French toast is rich and creamy in the center and crisp on the outside, with a healthy dose of good Southern bourbon to really give it flavor. Make sure to use thick bread that will hold the weight of the egg. Texas toast will work just fine. And, hey, go ahead and throw a few slices of thick country hickory-smoked bacon into the oven while you're at it.

4 large eggs
2 cups half-and-half
3 tablespoons bourbon
1 teaspoon pure vanilla extract
¼ cup light-brown sugar
1¼ teaspoons cinnamon
Pinch of kosher salt

Six 1-inch-thick slices brioche, challah bread, or from a nice pullman loaf
Nonstick spray
2 tablespoons unsalted butter, melted
Confectioners' sugar and maple syrup, for serving

In a medium bowl, whisk together eggs, half-and-half, bourbon, vanilla, brown sugar, cinnamon, and salt until they're blended and the sugar is dissolved.

Place bread in a single layer in a 13-by-9-inch casserole dish. Pour the wet mixture over the bread, and let soak for 15 minutes, flipping halfway through.

Heat a large griddle over medium heat. Spray with nonstick spray and brush with melted butter. Cook each slice of bread for 2 to 3 minutes per side, until golden brown. Don't overcrowd the griddle or the French toast won't brown evenly.

If cooking in batches, place cooked French toast on a wire-rack-lined sheet tray and keep warm in a 200-degree-F oven until ready to serve.

Dust with powdered sugar and drizzle with maple syrup before serving.

Serves 6

Breakfast Pot Pie

Gina There is nothing quite like this rustic breakfast pot pie. It's easy to serve, beautiful to present, and a great brunch dish. I love the fact that everything goes into one bowl—bacon, eggs, potatoes, and cheese (translation: less to clean). To cut time, you can use frozen hash browns, but I use the grater on my food processor to shred the potatoes, and it's just as easy. Slice it like a pie, and serve while it's still warm.

Nonstick spray

6 strips bacon, chopped

½ medium Vidalia onion, finely chopped

4 all-purpose potatoes (2 pounds), peeled, shredded, squeezed dry of excess water in a clean kitchen towel

4 large eggs plus 1 beaten egg, for egg wash

3 green onions, thinly sliced

½ cup half-and-half

Pinch of cayenne pepper

Kosher salt and freshly ground black pepper

1 cup shredded cheddar cheese

4 tablespoons unsalted butter, sliced into pats

All-purpose flour, for dusting

1 sheet frozen puff pastry (half of a 17.3-ounce package), thawed

Preheat oven to 400 degrees F. Adjust rack to lower third of oven.

Spray a 9½-inch deep-dish pie plate with nonstick spray.

Put bacon in a large skillet, and cook over medium heat, stirring, for 3 minutes, until some of the fat has rendered. Add the onion, and sauté until soft and just beginning to turn golden around the edges, about 8 minutes. Stir in the shredded potatoes and pat down in a single layer. Let brown slightly for 2 minutes. Use a spatula to flip, and brown again for 1 minute. Stir and break the potatoes up in the pan, cooking for another 2 minutes. Remove to a bowl, and cool.

Crack the eggs into a bowl, and add the green onions, half-and-half, cayenne, and salt and pepper. Beat with a whisk until blended.

Stir half of the cheese into the cooled potato mixture, then add to the prepared pie plate and pour the eggs over the top. Sprinkle the remaining cheese over the top, and add the pats of butter.

Dust your work surface with flour. Use a rolling pin to stretch out the puff pastry by an extra few inches to give room for crimping. Drape the puff pastry over the top of the filling. Fold and crimp the excess pastry within the edges of the pie dish. Use a knife to score the top in a crisscross pattern, then brush lightly with the beaten egg. Bake the pot pie for 40 to 45 minutes, until puffed and golden.

Serves 6 to 8

Griddled and Glazed Ham and Eggs

Pat Oh boy, do we love meat with our breakfast in the South. When I was growing up, it wasn't uncommon to walk into the kitchen and find Mama Rena frying a big piece of ham steak in her skillet. The steaks usually came from one of our relatives from the "country" who brought cuts of meat from their farm. You rarely see bone-in ham steaks on breakfast menus anymore, but I think there's still a place at the table for a good griddle ham-and-eggs breakfast. In our recipe, we glaze the ham with brown sugar. The pork is naturally salty on its own, so the only seasoning needed is paprika and cayenne to give it some spice. Include two runny eggs on the side, and this is a hearty breakfast worthy of any good Southerner.

¾ teaspoon light-brown sugar

¾ teaspoon smoked paprika

⅛ teaspoon cayenne pepper

⅛ teaspoon freshly ground black pepper, plus more for final seasoning

One 1-pound boneless ham steak

Nonstick spray

1 tablespoon salted butter

4 large eggs

Kosher salt

Buttered toast or biscuits, for serving

Heat a large griddle over medium-high heat.

Put the brown sugar, paprika, cayenne, and black pepper in a small bowl, and whisk to combine. Evenly sprinkle the mixture on both sides of the ham steak.

Coat the griddle lightly with nonstick spray, and add the butter. Once butter is melted and foamy, add the ham steak and cook until crisp, about 3 minutes per side. Remove the ham to a cutting board and cut into two equal pieces.

Crack the eggs onto the griddle, being careful not to break the yolks. Fry until the whites are set around the yolk and the edges are nice and golden-crisp, about 4 minutes. Season the eggs with salt and pepper.

Serve the eggs with the ham steak, and with buttered toast.

Serves 2 generously

Sausage Cream Gravy and Biscuits

Pat Everything's better with a little pig in it. Here's my proof: sausage cream gravy. You don't know Southern breakfast if you haven't had biscuits and gravy, and that's just what this recipe is, with a little pig mixed in. There's only one skillet you should use to make this dish, and that's cast iron, 'cause that's how we like to do it down here in Memphis.

¾ pound bulk breakfast
   sausage
¼ cup all-purpose flour
1½ cups whole milk
1 cup heavy cream

Kosher salt and freshly ground
   black pepper
Pinch of cayenne pepper
Easy Buttermilk and Cream Biscuits
   (page 15)

In a large cast-iron skillet, cook the sausage over medium heat, stirring and breaking it up with the back of a wooden spoon, until crumbly and browned, about 5 minutes. Sprinkle flour over the top of the sausage, and stir and cook for 2 minutes. Stir in the milk and cream, and bring to a boil. Reduce heat to a simmer, and cook for 5 minutes, until the mixture is thick. Season the gravy with salt, lots of black pepper, and a pinch of cayenne. Spoon the gravy over warm buttermilk biscuits.

Serves 8

Appetizers, Snacks, and Small Bites

Gina's Favorite Black-Eyed Pea Hummus with Pita Chips

Mini–Crab Cakes with Smoked Tomato Mayo

Memphis Caviar

Homemade Onion Dip with Old Bay Potato Chips

Pat's Spicy Hot Cheese Dip

Crunchy Fried Okra

Deep-Fried Pickles

Pepper Pig Candy

Gina's Hot Feta and Pimiento Cheese Spread

Fried Shrimp with Hot Pepper Jelly Dipping Sauce

Easy Brie-sy Baked Brie with Walnuts and Fresh Strawberry Jam

Homemade Fish Sticks with Tartar Sauce

Gina Although Pat and I are a couple, we have different tastes—especially in the kitchen. He likes food that's fried and spicy, whereas I prefer my fare lighter and sweet. That's the great thing about appetizers: you can serve a little something for everyone. Another tip: serve a big buffet of appetizers with one of my signature cocktails when you're entertaining. Instead of spending time in the kitchen making a big formal dinner, you can enjoy the party with everyone else!

Gina's Favorite Black-Eyed Pea Hummus with Pita Chips

Gina Whenever we were fussy about what we ate as kids, my mom would say, "Don't judge it by the way it looks." This is the case for me with hummus. I will openly and freely admit that the first time I saw a bowl of hummus I wanted nothing to do with it. But once I realized chickpeas are similar to black-eyed peas, I not only decided to give hummus a try, I took it one step further and invented my own down-home version of the dip, made with black-eyed peas. In my version, I leave out the tahini and throw in smoked paprika, cumin, and cayenne to punch up the spiciness just enough to make all the flavors pop.

Two 15-ounce cans black-eyed peas, drained and rinsed
2 cloves garlic, smashed and peeled
Zest and juice of 1 lemon
¼ cup cold water
¼ cup olive oil
1 teaspoon sesame oil

½ teaspoon smoked paprika
⅛ teaspoon ground cumin
Pinch of cayenne pepper
Kosher salt and freshly ground black pepper
Pita Chips (see sidebar) or cut-up vegetables, for serving

In a food processor, combine the black-eyed peas, garlic, lemon zest and juice, water, olive oil, sesame oil, paprika, cumin, cayenne, and salt and pepper, and purée until blended and smooth. Serve with pita chips or vegetable crudités.

Makes 1½ cups, serving 4 to 6

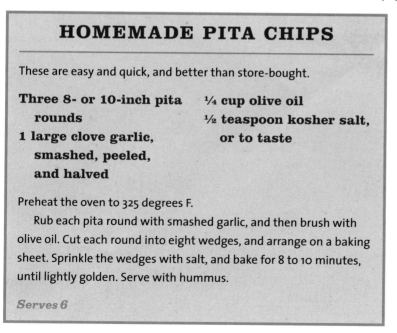

HOMEMADE PITA CHIPS

These are easy and quick, and better than store-bought.

Three 8- or 10-inch pita rounds
1 large clove garlic, smashed, peeled, and halved

¼ cup olive oil
½ teaspoon kosher salt, or to taste

Preheat the oven to 325 degrees F.

Rub each pita round with smashed garlic, and then brush with olive oil. Cut each round into eight wedges, and arrange on a baking sheet. Sprinkle the wedges with salt, and bake for 8 to 10 minutes, until lightly golden. Serve with hummus.

Serves 6

Mini–Crab Cakes with Smoked Tomato Mayo

Pat I didn't eat much seafood growing up. I was one of six children, and in those days we didn't have much money. It was hard to keep a family of six children full on seafood, so my mom often made heartier dishes like chicken, roasts, and pork. It wasn't until recently, when Gina, Spenser, and Shelbi started demanding more seafood, that I was encouraged to try crab-cake sandwiches. In this recipe we're making mini-sandwiches, but if you're alone and want to make one big sandwich, who am I to stop you?

Smoked Tomato Mayo, for serving
   (recipe follows)
¼ cup mayonnaise
1 teaspoon Dijon mustard
⅛ teaspoon cayenne pepper
1 large egg, beaten
Juice of ½ lemon

Dash of hot sauce
Dash of Worcestershire sauce
Kosher salt and freshly ground
   black pepper
¾ cup panko breadcrumbs
1 pound lump crabmeat
¼ cup peanut oil, for frying

Make the smoked-tomato mayo and refrigerate. The mayo mixture will thicken up and become much more flavorful the longer it chills.

In a separate bowl, stir together the plain mayonnaise, mustard, cayenne, egg, lemon juice, hot sauce, Worcestershire sauce, and salt and pepper.

In another bowl sprinkle the panko over the crab, and add the mayonnaise mixture. Gently fold all the ingredients together, making sure not to break up any of the large crab lumps. Divide the batter using a ¼-cup measure, and then form into eleven cakes. Place the cakes on a sheet tray, cover with plastic wrap, and refrigerate for 30 minutes.

Heat the peanut oil in a cast-iron skillet over medium-high heat. Cook the crab cakes about 4 minutes on each side, until golden and brown. Drain on a paper-towel-lined plate. Serve with Smoked Tomato Mayo.

Serves 4 to 6

Smoked Tomato Mayo

1 plum tomato, sliced in half
1 slice red onion, 1 inch thick
2 teaspoons olive oil
Kosher salt and freshly ground
   black pepper

1 cup mayonnaise
¼ teaspoon smoked paprika

Heat a grill or grill pan over medium-high heat.

Coat the tomato and onion with olive oil, and season with salt and pepper. Grill tomato and onion for 4 minutes on each side, or until charred and soft. Let cool.

Process the tomato, onion, mayonnaise, smoked paprika, and salt and pepper together in a food processor until smooth. Remove to a bowl, cover with plastic wrap, and refrigerate for 30 minutes before serving.

Makes about 1¼ cups

Memphis Caviar

Gina This is the best party dish I have ever made, for several reasons: you can make it the night before, it displays beautifully, and the recipe yields a big batch, which means lots of leftovers. Not only is this dish colorful, but the textures are amazing and the flavor will knock your socks off. To take it up a notch, use our pickled peppers (page 9) in place of the red jalapeño. Caviar anyone?

Two 15-ounce cans black-eyed peas, drained and rinsed

¼ medium red onion, finely chopped

1 plum tomato, finely chopped

1 small yellow bell pepper, seeded and finely chopped

1 red jalapeño, seeded and finely chopped (or Pickled Peppers, page 9)

3 green onions, sliced

2 cloves garlic, finely chopped

¼ cup red-wine vinegar

2 tablespoons olive oil

½ teaspoon red-pepper flakes

¼ teaspoon ground cumin

¼ cup finely chopped fresh parsley

Kosher salt and freshly ground black pepper

Tortilla chips, for serving

In a large bowl, combine the black-eyed peas, onion, tomato, peppers, and green onions. In a smaller bowl, whisk together the garlic, vinegar, olive oil, red-pepper flakes, cumin, parsley, and salt and pepper. Toss everything together, and season with a big pinch of salt and pepper. Cover with plastic wrap, and refrigerate at least 2 hours, preferably overnight, before serving. Serve with tortilla chips.

Serves 6 to 8

Homemade Onion Dip with Old Bay Potato Chips

Pat Onion dip was very popular in the 1970s, but in my father's family this dip has much deeper roots. My grandmother always served it at social gatherings, like her Saturday afternoon card games, and as a kid, my father used to sneak tastes when no one was looking. As he grew older, onion dip became his favorite snack food to have while watching ball games. Now, understand, he couldn't make toast and always burned the popcorn, so the way he cooked dip was by pouring mix from a packet into sour cream, 1970s-style. I created this homemade version in his honor.

My version is made with big, juicy, sweet Georgia Vidalia onions, and I add a little kick with a dash of hot sauce and Worcestershire sauce. But, listen, you can't serve this memorial dip with some ole store-bought chips. So, hell, we'll make our own. (Just don't cook them like Daddy used to cook his popcorn.)

---

2 tablespoons olive oil
3 medium Vidalia onions, chopped
2 cloves garlic, finely chopped
One 8-ounce package cream cheese, at room temperature
¾ cup sour cream
¼ cup mayonnaise
¼ cup sliced fresh chives

2 tablespoons finely chopped fresh parsley
Dash of hot sauce
Dash of Worcestershire sauce
Kosher salt and freshly ground back pepper
Old Bay Potato Chips, for serving (recipe follows)

Place a large heavy-bottomed skillet over medium-high heat, and add the oil. Once it's hot, add the onions and reduce heat to medium. Cook the onions, stirring occasionally, until they are very soft and caramelized, about 50 to 55 minutes. Add the garlic for the last minute of sautéing, and cook until fragrant, about 1 minute. Remove from heat, and let cool.

Combine the cream cheese, sour cream, and mayonnaise in a bowl. Whip with an electric hand mixer until smooth and creamy, about 3 minutes. Toss in chives, parsley, hot sauce, and Worcestershire sauce, and beat until incorporated. Fold in the cooled onion mixture, and taste for seasoning. Add salt and pepper to taste. Enjoy with Old Bay Potato Chips.

Makes 3 cups, serving 4 to 6

CHARLES M. BLOW
Blind to the Past
Don't use a ladder
MORE OP-ED
OLD B
SEASON

Old Bay Potato Chips

Peanut oil, for frying
2 large russet potatoes (about 1 pound),
  well scrubbed

1 to 2 tablespoons Old Bay Seasoning,
  according to taste

Preheat 4 inches of peanut oil in a deep-fryer or a heavy-bottomed Dutch oven to 375 degrees F.

Using a mandoline outfitted with a straight-blade attachment, slice the potatoes into ⅛-inch-thick rounds. Add potatoes to a large bowl of cold water, and swish them around. Drain potatoes well, and pat dry with paper towels.

Fry the potatoes in batches, for about 3 minutes, until crisp and deeply golden. Remove the chips from the fryer, and pour onto a towel-lined tray. Season with Old Bay immediately, while the chips are still oily (this helps the seasoning stick to the chips).

Serves 4 to 6

Pat's Spicy Hot Cheese Dip

Pat There ain't nothing like a good homemade dip. In our neck of the woods, we like ours warm and cheesy. Even when Gina and my girls try to tell me they're not hungry, they can't keep their damn chips out of my dip! I actually thought that, by using hot sauce and pepper jack, I was making it too hot for them. No chance. The butter and milk smooth this dip out perfectly, so, whether the guys are coming over for a big game or you're just hanging with your girls, this dip will win over everyone's palate.

---

2 tablespoons unsalted butter
½ medium red onion, chopped
2 jalapeños, seeded and chopped
2 tablespoons all-purpose flour
1½ cups whole milk
1½ cups shredded pepper-jack cheese
1½ cups shredded part-skim mozzarella

1 plum tomato, seeded and chopped
Juice of 1 lime
¼ teaspoon chili powder
Big dash of hot sauce
Big dash of Worcestershire sauce
Bagel chips, for serving

In a large saucepan, heat the butter over medium-high heat. Once it's melted and foamy, toss in the onion and jalapeños, and sauté until soft, about 5 minutes. Stir in the flour and stir for a few minutes, until pasty and golden. While stirring, pour in the milk, and cook until the sauce is thick, about 3 minutes. Turn heat to medium low, and add the cheese by handfuls, stirring well between additions, until all the cheese is completely melted. Add the chopped tomato, lime juice, chili powder, hot sauce, and Worcestershire sauce, and stir until everything is well combined. Serve immediately with bagel chips.

Serves 4 to 6

Crunchy Fried Okra

Pat Okra is a quick-growing vegetable that thrives in warm weather. Versatile in the kitchen, it can be used as a thickener in stews and gumbos, pickled, fried, sautéed, or boiled. Mama Rena (my dad's mom) grew okra in her garden when I was growing up, and when I say it was plentiful, I mean she served it for dinner at least three times a week. I was never a fan of boiled okra, and she knew it, so she made a special fried version just for me. I've copied her recipe and added a little spice of my own (what, you thought I wouldn't?). The cayenne and black pepper add a bite of flavor, while the buttermilk and hot sauce coated with cornmeal contribute the required crunch. Put it all together and you have a vegetable that even the pickiest eaters will love.

Peanut oil, for frying
1 cup low-fat buttermilk
1 tablespoon hot sauce
Big dash of Worcestershire sauce
1 cup all-purpose flour
1 cup yellow cornmeal

½ teaspoon cayenne pepper
½ teaspoon granulated garlic
Kosher salt and freshly ground
   black pepper
1 pound okra, trimmed and
   cut into ¼-inch rounds

Heat a deep-fryer or a large cast-iron skillet filled halfway with oil to 350 degrees F.

Combine the buttermilk, hot sauce, and Worcestershire sauce in a large bowl. In another bowl, whisk together the flour, cornmeal, cayenne, garlic, and salt and pepper. Add the okra to the bowl with the buttermilk, and swish around to soak completely. Remove the okra from the buttermilk, let the excess drip away, and then toss the okra in the cornmeal mixture to coat. Add the okra to the hot oil in batches and fry until crisp and crunchy, 4 to 5 minutes. Drain well on a paper-towel-lined sheet tray, and season while still hot with a big pinch of salt.

Serves 4

Deep-Fried Pickles

Pat When I was a kid, every corner store sold big dill pickles for a quarter apiece. The fun part was to look through the sides of the jar and tell the store owner which pickle you wanted. This always frustrated the hell out of him. He would say, "Son, they're all the same size." I would respond, "No, sir, Mr. Johnson, that one right there [using my finger to point] has my name on it." He was a grumpy old man and would grumble jokingly as he worked his fork into the jar to pull out the one I wanted. Of course, one of the best ways to eat pickles is to fry them. The key to the best fried pickles is firm pickle slices and hot, hot oil. The paprika and cayenne pepper in this recipe add a smoky kick, and the dredging is a layering of flour, egg, flour, then breadcrumbs. These pickles would've kept Mr. Johnson's business booming!

Peanut oil, for frying
One 11-ounce jar dill-pickle slices,
    well drained
½ cup whole milk
2 large eggs
1¼ cups all-purpose flour, divided

½ cup breadcrumbs
1 teaspoon paprika
¾ teaspoon cayenne pepper
Kosher salt and freshly ground
    black pepper
Ranch dressing, for serving

Fill a large heavy-bottomed pot or a deep-fryer halfway with peanut oil, and heat to 350 degrees F.

Drain the pickles in a colander in the sink.

Whisk together the milk and eggs in a medium bowl. In a separate bowl, whisk together ½ cup flour, breadcrumbs, paprika, cayenne, and a big pinch of salt and pepper. In a third bowl, put ¾ cup flour. Dredge the pickles first through the plain flour, then through the wet ingredients. Let the excess egg mixture drip off, and toss pickles in the flour-and-breadcrumb mixture. Fry the pickles in batches until golden and brown, about 2 minutes. Remove to a paper-towel-lined sheet tray, and season while hot with a big pinch of salt. Serve with ranch dressing.

Serves 6

MAMA RENA (Irene Wright)

Pat I remember my father's mother, Mama Rena, as a beautiful woman, with long silky gray hair. Photos of her as a young woman reveal she was always that gorgeous. She was born into a large family, with eight or nine sisters. Her father was a sharecropper, and you can imagine, with so many women in the house, that there was a lot of cooking going on in their kitchen. Mama Rena was physically a small woman, but she had an extremely large presence in the kitchen, and she cooked seven days a week. I never remember seeing canned goods or boxed ingredients on her shelves. Everything was made from scratch.

She and my grandfather lived in a modest home with a huge backyard. Cornered off in a small section of that yard was an area fenced in with chicken wire. This garden was Mama Rena's special place. She grew cabbage, okra, greens, and tomatoes, and tended it very well. She was out there at least once a week, carefully pulling weeds, watering, and harvesting. Mama Rena's specialties were stew, catfish, soups, and veggies. And in the summertime she made the best homemade ice cream you could ever imagine, flavored with fresh fruits, like peaches or strawberries.

A true Southern "church lady," Mama Rena attended church every Sunday with her Bible, wearing her best Sunday dress and fancy hat. In those days, Southern Baptist church services lasted for several hours, and Mama Rena never wanted dinner to be late. So she used to wake up around 4 a.m. on Sundays to prepare breakfast and start dinner before getting dressed for church. When I spent the weekend with her, I would wake up to flavorful smells, and the windows in her tiny kitchen would be fogged. I guess her kitchen was too hot!

She loved my father, and after his passing she continued to show her love for him by caring for his children. There was nothing she wouldn't do for us, including putting her house up for a loan so that we could open our first restaurant. When I stopped by her house for a visit on my own, I would often find her sitting in her favorite chair in the living room. As soon as I walked in, the first words out of her mouth were "Are you hungry, old man?" And of course I would say, "Yes, Mama!"

Pepper Pig Candy

Gina Now, you all know I love pigs. They are everywhere in my home, and I've made everything from pig-themed cocktails (Pigatinis) to Christmas-tree ornaments. You know I also love me some cayenne pepper (I sing its praises on the show all the time). I've been thinking about how to combine my two favorites in one dish, and this recipe was inspired by the bacon we serve at our restaurant in New York. It's important to use slab bacon, because you need the thickness to support the brown sugar, ground ginger, cayenne, and black pepper. Season the bacon, put it in the oven, and there you have it: Pepper Pig. Eat it alone, or use it as garnish in a cocktail. Either way, it's smokin'!

⅓ cup packed light-brown sugar
½ teaspoon cayenne pepper
¼ teaspoon freshly ground black pepper

¼ teaspoon ground ginger
8 strips thick-cut bacon

Preheat oven to 350 degrees F, and adjust oven rack to center. Line a baking sheet with heavy-duty foil, and fit with a wire baking rack.

Mix together the brown sugar, cayenne, black pepper, and ground ginger in a medium bowl. Toss in the bacon, one strip at a time, and make sure it gets nicely coated with the sugar mixture. Put bacon strips in a single layer on the wire rack, and sprinkle any sugar left in the bowl on top. Bake for 25 minutes, until candied and crisp. Let cool for 5 minutes before serving.

Serves 6 to 8

Gina's Hot Feta and Pimiento Cheese Spread

Gina I can't recall a time when pimiento-cheese sandwiches weren't popular (for good reason—they were first made over 100 years ago!), and they're still found at luncheons across the South. The original recipe always called for cheddar cheese, pimientos, and mayonnaise, with some variation of seasonings added. When I thought about updating it, I realized that my favorite cheese, feta, had enough creaminess to replace the mayo and enough bite to replace the sharp cheddar. I turned it into a hot dip by topping the feta with the pimientos and sautéed red and yellow tomatoes. You can either bake the entire dish or, if you prefer to keep it as a spread, just mix it all together once the tomato-and-pimiento mixture has cooled.

2 tablespoons olive oil

3 cloves garlic, chopped

1½ cups yellow and red cherry tomatoes, sliced in half (¾ cup)

One 2-ounce jar diced pimientos, drained

Dash of hot sauce

Kosher salt and freshly ground black pepper

7-ounce slab feta cheese

Crostini or crustless white-bread slices, for serving

Preheat oven to 350 degrees F.

In a medium skillet, heat olive oil over medium-high heat. Once it's hot, add the garlic, and sauté until fragrant and just beginning to turn gold around the edges. Stir in tomatoes and cook, stirring, until the tomatoes have begun to break down, 4 to 5 minutes. Toss in the pimientos, add a glug of hot sauce, and season with a pinch of salt and pepper. Remove from heat.

Put feta in a 12-ounce oval gratin dish, and pour the saucy pimientos and tomatoes over the top. Bake for 20 minutes, until bubbly. Serve as a dip with crostini, or take it old-school Southern and serve it as a spread on finger sandwiches.

Serves 4

Fried Shrimp with Hot Pepper Jelly Dipping Sauce

Gina Remember the Hot Pepper Jelly we introduced you to in the first chapter? We told you that jelly could be used in a lot of different dishes, and this recipe is proof. Fried shrimp always remind me of "Nawlins" (New Orleans), but this recipe has enough buttermilk, cornmeal, and paprika to keep it true to Memphis.

Peanut oil, for frying
1 cup buttermilk
1 large egg, lightly beaten
1 tablespoon Creole mustard
1 tablespoon hot sauce
½ cup self-rising flour
½ cup yellow cornmeal
2 teaspoons paprika

2 teaspoons kosher salt
1 teaspoon cayenne pepper
1 teaspoon garlic powder
1½ pounds large shrimp, peeled and deveined
Lemon wedges, for serving
Hot Pepper Jelly Dipping Sauce (recipe follows)

Fill a countertop deep-fryer halfway with peanut oil and heat to 375 degrees F. Or use a large heavy-bottomed saucepan outfitted with a deep-fry thermometer and filled with peanut oil 3 inches deep.

Whisk together the buttermilk, egg, mustard, and hot sauce in a casserole dish. In a second casserole dish, whisk together flour, cornmeal, paprika, salt, cayenne, and garlic powder.

Dredge the shrimp in the flour mixture, then in the egg mixture, then back through the flour again, making sure the excess drips off. Fry in batches until crisp and golden brown, about 2 minutes per batch. Drain on a paper-towel-lined sheet tray.

Serve with pepper-jelly dipping sauce and lemon wedges on the side.

Serves 4 to 6

Hot Pepper Jelly Dipping Sauce

¾ cup Hot Pepper Jelly (page 6)   2 tablespoons rice-wine vinegar

---

Combine ingredients together in a small bowl.

Makes about 1 cup

Easy Brie-sy Baked Brie with Walnuts and Fresh Strawberry Jam

Gina My great-grandmother Callie used to serve Brie as a light snack while she hosted catch-up (gossip) gatherings with her friends in the parlor. I'd grab a cracker, spread some Brie, and try to eavesdrop on the chatter. Until she caught me, of course—and she always did. "Girl, stop looking in my mouth before a word knocks you in the head!" she'd say. With or without the gossip, this dip always reminds me of my great-grandmother and afternoons in the parlor. Served with crackers and some ripe strawberries, it's the perfect spring treat.

---

1 small (8-ounce) round of Brie cheese
1 cup fresh Small Batch Strawberry Jam
   (page 5)

2 tablespoons toasted and salted
   walnuts, roughly chopped
Crackers and strawberries, for serving

Preheat oven to 350 degrees F.

Place the Brie on a sheet tray. Bake for 20 minutes, until the Brie is melted and oozy to the touch. Carefully remove the hot Brie to a serving dish with a spatula. Top the Brie round with the jam, and sprinkle with chopped walnuts. Serve with crackers and strawberries.

Serves 6

Homemade Fish Sticks with Tartar Sauce

Gina When I was younger, I used to love coming home from school and making myself fish sticks as an after-school snack. I remember pulling the packaged fish sticks out of the freezer, laying them on a sheet tray, and making the tartar sauce from the little enclosed packet. Oh, the good ole days. This time around, there won't be a box, and we're using fresh cod. We substitute panko breadcrumbs for the cornmeal and add a bit of a kick of cayenne pepper and garlic (a great seasoning combination for most fish). All you have to do is a little dredging, and, trust me, the effort is worth it. The tartar sauce is just four ingredients: mayo, pickled relish, hot sauce, and yellow mustard. Yep, I think we beat the packet.

Nonstick spray

1¼ pounds cod fillets, skinless and boneless, cut into strips about 3 inches long and 1 inch wide

Kosher salt and freshly ground black pepper

½ cup all-purpose flour

2 teaspoons garlic powder

⅛ teaspoon cayenne pepper

2 large eggs, beaten

1½ cups panko breadcrumbs

¼ cup grated Parmesan cheese

1 tablespoon finely chopped fresh parsley

Tartar Sauce, for serving (recipe follows)

Preheat oven to 475 degrees F. Place a wire rack inside a rimmed baking sheet, and spray with nonstick spray. Season the cod with salt and pepper on both sides.

Whisk together the flour, garlic powder, and cayenne in a rimmed baking dish or pie plate. Put the beaten eggs in a second pie plate. In a third pie plate, whisk together the panko, Parmesan cheese, chopped parsley, and a pinch of salt and pepper. Dredge the fish sticks through the flour, the eggs (allowing the excess to drip off), and then into the panko mixture. Arrange the fish on the prepared rack, and lightly spritz with nonstick spray. Bake until golden and crisp, 15 to 17 minutes. Serve with the tartar sauce.

Serves 4

Tartar Sauce

½ cup mayonnaise

¼ cup Sweet Pickled Relish
  (page 10, or store-bought)

1 teaspoon hot sauce

½ teaspoon yellow mustard

Mix all the ingredients together, and refrigerate for 20 minutes before serving.

Makes about ¾ cup

Stewed Pinto Beans

Roasted Winter Root Vegetables

Roasted Broccoli with Cheddar Cheese Sauce

Butter Boiled Corn and Red Potatoes with Creole Seasoning

Grilled Succotash

Gina's Quick Confetti Collards

Mashed Cauliflower with Cheddar and Chives

Side Dishes, Veggies, and Salads

Charred Vegetable Salad with Grilled Croutons

Roasted Fingerling Potatoes with Fresh Herbs

Spicy Tomato Stewed Greens

Black-Eyed Pea Cakes

Cheesy Double Stuffed Potatoes

Summer Green Bean and Barley Salad

Shake It Up Salad with Basil Buttermilk Dressing

Kale Salad with Chopped Almonds, Feta, and Champagne Vinaigrette

Not Your Basic Sweet Potato Salad

Vinegar Slaw

Grilled Steak Salad with Bacon and Blue Cheese

Broccoli Slaw

Picnic Rice Salad

Pat Side dishes are often thought of as fillers around the main dish, but I think our grandparents and mothers put more thought and effort into the side dishes than they gave the actual entrée. As a child, I remember walking into their kitchens and noticing several smaller pots cooking on the stovetop, each filled with a different dish. The aroma was incredible. Mama Daisy was known for her famous black-eyed peas and oven-roasted root vegetables. Mama Rena made the best slaw, outstanding boiled corn, and colorful garden salads. My mom was influenced by both of them and perfected her pinto beans, collard greens, broccoli, and green beans.

Gina and I are grateful that these women are a part of our heritage, and we're proud to inherit the recipes and techniques. We put the lessons they taught us to work in this chapter—with our own twists, of course. You're going to go crazy over our Mashed Cauliflower with Cheddar and Chives, and Gina's Quick Confetti Collards and Kale Salad are fresh takes on classic side dishes. Y'all know I'm a steak-and-potato man, so we included our Grilled Steak Salad and our Roasted Fingerling Potatoes with Fresh Herbs. There is something for everyone in this chapter, and we hope you share these recipes with your loved ones just as we do.

Stewed Pinto Beans

Pat Every now and then you have to dig deep into the family recipe book and pull out an old Southern dish that has been passed down for generations. For our family, this means pinto beans. My mom used to cook big pots of them, enough to fill up five growing and hungry boys. She would always add a dash of sweet pickled relish on top to sweeten it all up, so we would clean our plates. I remember my mom used chunks of meat in her recipe, and I tried to incorporate that into my version as well. Gina makes fun of me for turning every dish into a stew. Well, I love me some stew! To me, pinto beans are no fun hanging out by themselves, but throw in a few chopped veggies, some homemade chicken broth, and some good old browned pork ribs, and you have a meal. When I really want to bring back memories of home, I add a spoonful of pickled relish just to my serving ('cause the girls don't know nothing about that).

---

1 pound dried pinto beans

2 tablespoons vegetable oil

1 pound boneless pork country ribs

Kosher salt and freshly ground
  black pepper

1 medium onion, chopped

1 green bell pepper, seeded and chopped

3 cloves garlic, chopped

1 teaspoon cayenne pepper

½ teaspoon smoked paprika

4 cups homemade or store-bought
  low-sodium chicken broth

1 dried bay leaf

Big dash of hot sauce

Sweet Pickled Relish (optional),
  for serving (page 10)

Sort through the beans, discarding any that look shriveled and removing any dirt or small stones. Put the remaining beans in a large pot, and cover with water by 2 inches. Bring them to a boil and cook for 2 minutes, then remove from the heat. Cover the pot, and leave the beans to soak in the hot water for 1 hour. Drain and rinse.

Heat the oil in a large heavy-bottomed pot over medium heat. Season ribs with salt and pepper. When the oil is shimmering, add the ribs. Cook until the pork is well browned on all sides, 4 minutes on each side. Remove the pork to a plate. Add the onion, bell pepper, and garlic to the pot, and cook for 5 minutes, until everything is soft and just beginning to brown. Stir in the cayenne and paprika, and cook for 30 seconds. Add the chicken broth, the pork and any leftover juice on the plate, the beans, and the bay leaf. Cook, covered, for 1½ hours, stirring on occasion.

After 1½ hours, remove the lid, check to make sure the beans are soft, and turn up the heat to medium high. Cook for an additional 25 to 30 minutes, until the liquid is reduced, the beans are very soft, and the meat is falling apart. Remove the bay leaf, and, if needed, break up the meat and partially mash the beans in the pot with a wooden spoon. Taste for seasoning, add hot sauce as desired, and serve with pickled relish on top.

Serves 6 to 8 (or 4 as a main dish)

Roasted Winter Root Vegetables

Gina When our daughter Shelbi was younger, she stayed with Mama Callie and Nana while Pat and I were working. I can still see them in Nana's backyard garden, teaching Shelbi how to pull the root vegetables out of the ground, then clean and prepare them. It wasn't long until Shelbi was picking greens and drinking coffee like an old soul. They'd take the veggies into the house, toss them in olive oil, and season them lightly. There isn't any update that could make this recipe better, so I left it exactly as it was, and exactly as it should be.

---

3 medium red potatoes, scrubbed
   and quartered
1 parsnip, peeled and cut into
   2-inch pieces
1 rutabaga, peeled and cut into
   2-inch pieces
2 carrots, peeled and cut into
   2-inch pieces

1 large red onion, cut into eighths
3 tablespoons olive oil
Kosher salt and freshly ground
   black pepper
Pinch of red-pepper flakes
1 tablespoon chopped fresh parsley

Preheat oven to 425 degrees F. Place the potatoes, parsnip, rutabaga, carrots, and red onion on a rimmed sheet tray. Drizzle with olive oil, and season with salt, pepper, and red-pepper flakes. Toss well together, making sure all the veggies are coated in oil and in a single layer. Roast for 45 to 50 minutes, until golden brown and cooked through. Sprinkle chopped parsley on top for a pop of green.

Serves 4 to 6

Roasted Broccoli with Cheddar Cheese Sauce

Pat There was a time when broccoli was the only vegetable Gina and I could get Spenser (our older daughter) to eat. So, of course, we had to get creative. For a long time, we would simply boil some water and blanch the broccoli, but she absolutely fell in love once we started roasting it. Roasting condenses the flavor of the broccoli, and the olive oil really helps the red pepper and seasoning stick to each floret.

---

2 medium broccoli crowns, cut into 2-inch-long florets
¼ cup olive oil
Pinch of red-pepper flakes
Kosher salt and freshly ground black pepper

2 tablespoons salted butter
2 cloves garlic, roughly chopped
2 tablespoons all-purpose flour
1 cup low-fat milk
1 cup grated sharp cheddar cheese

Preheat oven to 450 degrees F.

Pile the broccoli on a rimmed sheet tray, and toss with olive oil, red-pepper flakes, and salt and pepper. Place in the oven, and roast for 15 to 18 minutes, until the florets are crisp and lightly golden brown.

While the broccoli roasts, start the cheese sauce. Over medium heat, melt the butter in a medium saucepan until slightly foamy. Add the garlic, and cook until fragrant, about 1 minute. Stir in flour, and cook until the mixture is pasty and blond in color, about 3 minutes. Whisk in the milk, and bring to a simmer. Cook, while stirring, until the mixture is thick. Add the cheese in handfuls, stirring until each addition is completely melted.

Remove broccoli from oven, put in a serving dish, and pour cheese sauce over the top. Serve immediately.

Serves 4 to 6

Butter Boiled Corn and Red Potatoes with Creole Seasoning

Pat Red potatoes are one of our younger daughter Shelbi's favorites, and she always used to ask if I could cook them with the skins on. This is a dish she'd love, because we're going to do just that, and add hot buttered corn and Creole seasoning (a spice blend that usually consists of paprika, cayenne, onion powder, garlic powder, oregano, and thyme).

---

2 ears corn, shucked and cut into thirds
4 medium red potatoes, cut into
   chunks
2 teaspoons Creole seasoning

Kosher salt and freshly ground
   black pepper
4 tablespoons unsalted butter,
   sliced into pats

Combine the corn and potatoes in a large saucepan, and cover with cold water. Stir in the Creole seasoning and a big pinch of salt. Bring to a boil, then reduce to a simmer and cook until potatoes are very tender, about 20 minutes. (We cook the potatoes until they are on the verge of falling apart—they are more than just fork-tender.) Drain the veggies, and place in a serving bowl. Top with pats of butter, a dash more Creole seasoning, and salt and pepper.

Serves 4 to 6

Grilled Succotash

Pat This old Southern dish has been around a long time. A great succotash must include lima beans, corn, onions, tomatoes, and fresh basil. I haven't seen succotash grilled before, but it's a great way to introduce a smoky, charred flavor to the dish. Toss with a light coating of Lemon Vinaigrette and you have the perfect summer salad.

2 cups fresh or frozen shelled
   lima beans
3 ears corn, shucked
1 zucchini, cut on the bias into
   ⅓-inch slices
½ red onion, sliced into
   ⅓-inch-thick rings
2 tablespoons olive oil
Kosher salt and freshly ground
   black pepper
1 cup cherry tomatoes,
   sliced in half

¼ cup fresh basil, roughly
   chopped

LEMON VINAIGRETTE
1 teaspoon Dijon mustard
Juice of 1 lemon
Kosher salt and freshly ground
   black pepper
¼ cup olive oil

Heat grill to medium-high heat.

Pour the lima beans into a pot of boiling salted water, and cook for 12 minutes, or until soft. Drain in a colander, and rinse with cold water to stop the cooking.

Place the corn, zucchini, and red onion on a sheet tray, and drizzle with the olive oil. Season with salt and pepper, and toss well together, making sure all the veggies are coated in oil and seasoned well with salt and pepper. Grill the corn until lightly charred on all sides, about 6 minutes. Grill zucchini and onions on both sides until lightly charred and soft, 4 to 5 minutes total. Remove from grill, and cool slightly.

Chop the zucchini and onion into bite-sized pieces. With a chef's knife, cut the corn kernels from the cob. Use the back of your blade to scrape against the cob to press out the milky liquid. Put the chopped veggies, the corn, and its milk in a large bowl, and toss in the tomatoes and basil.

Whisk together the mustard, lemon juice, and salt and pepper in a small bowl. Drizzle in the olive oil, and whisk well until emulsified. Pour dressing over salad, and toss. Taste and adjust seasonings if necessary.

Serves 4 to 6

Gina's Quick Confetti Collards

Gina Give me collards, collards, and more collards! I have done everything with collards except, until now, cutting them into ribbon confetti (see Tip below). Once that's done, you're just a quick sauté away from completing the dish. How can you beat that? This dish is best served hot, so make it the last thing you prepare.

---

1 large bundle collard greens,
    well washed
2 tablespoons olive oil
4 cloves garlic, finely chopped

¼ teaspoon red-pepper flakes
Kosher salt and freshly ground
    black pepper
½ lemon

Fold the collard leaves in half and cut out and discard the exposed center ribs and stems. Stack four leaves on top of each other, and roll tightly into a cylinder. Slice the collards into thin ribbons, about ¼ inch thick. Repeat with the remaining leaves.

Heat olive oil in a large skillet over medium-high heat. When the oil is hot, add the garlic and red-pepper flakes, and quickly sauté until just fragrant, about 30 seconds. Add the collard greens, by handfuls, and toss quickly with tongs in the hot oil for 3 to 4 minutes. Season with salt and pepper, and give the greens a big squeeze of lemon juice. Continue cooking until the lemon juice has evaporated, about 30 seconds. Serve hot.

Serves 4

Tip I always prefer fresh collard leaves. If you like, you can wash and ribbon them the night before and store them in the refrigerator; just place a damp paper towel over the top of the cut collards so they don't get wimpy. Nobody likes a wimpy collard.

Mashed Cauliflower with Cheddar and Chives

Gina If you're not cooking with cauliflower, you are missing out. In the South, cauliflower is often baked into casseroles, but it also works boiled, fried, steamed, or just eaten raw. In this recipe, we've transformed it into something just as tasty as good old mashed potatoes.

---

1 large head cauliflower, cored and
   roughly chopped
Kosher salt and freshly ground
   black pepper
2 tablespoons unsalted butter
2 cloves garlic, finely chopped
¼ cup whole milk

½ cup shredded sharp cheddar cheese
2 ounces cream cheese, cut into
   small pieces
¼ cup sour cream
4 tablespoons sliced fresh chives,
   divided

Fill a large saucepan with water, and bring to a boil over medium-high heat. Add the cauliflower and a big pinch of salt. Cook for 10 to 12 minutes, or until tender. Drain cauliflower in a colander.

Place the pot you cooked the cauliflower in back on the stovetop over medium heat. Put in the butter, and once it's melted and foamy, add the garlic and sauté until fragrant, about 1 minute. Add the milk; when it's steaming, turn off the heat. Add the cauliflower, and give it a good mash with a wooden spoon. Stir in the cheddar, cream cheese, and sour cream. Spoon the mixture into a food processor, and pulse until smooth. Add 3 tablespoons of the chives, and give 2 more pulses (make sure not to overblend and turn the mash into a green mess!).

Place the mashed cauliflower in a serving bowl, and sprinkle with the remaining tablespoon of chives.

Serves 4 to 6

PAT'S MOM (Lorine Neely)

Pat My mom had six kids. I can only imagine what it must have been like trying to plan meals. I'm next to the youngest, so I wasn't that involved in helping her in the kitchen until my siblings got older and started to move out. She told me most of her cooking skills came from her mother, who demanded that she spend time with her in the kitchen. So she did the same for me, and thank God. She has shared so many wonderful recipes, dishes, and stories: stews, pot roast, spaghetti, lasagna, collard greens, pinto beans, and chicken were her specialties. She married my father out of high school at seventeen, and had her first child at eighteen—that's not a lot of time to adjust! Mama Rena taught her how to prepare certain dishes that my father loved, and one of his favorites was the pork-chop soup from our first cookbook (*Down Home with the Neelys*). It's hard to believe that that recipe is almost ninety years old. My mother has since passed it down to me, and I'm still making it for the girls. Maybe one day they will prepare it for my grandchildren.

My mom didn't have cookbooks to consult to create new and different dishes for us, but she had something more valuable: a tin box with index cards in it. These were handwritten recipes that she had gathered from her mom and mother-in-law. She and my father moved to Michigan a few years after getting married, but she would often call back to Memphis to gather these generational recipes, write them on index cards, and place them in her tin box. I wish I could get ahold of that tin box (I'm sure there are at least two best-selling cookbooks in there!), but over the years, and after several moves, it's been misplaced. And of course, after you prepare a dish a few times, you don't need to rely as heavily on the cards for recipes and directions. My mom has so many cooking habits and techniques that come directly from my grandparents. I'm just so lucky that they have been passed down to me.

Charred Vegetable Salad with Grilled Croutons

Pat Every time Gina asks if there's anything I won't grill, I always reply, "ice cream." Of course, then I get that familiar look, which isn't good. I love grilling zucchini and squash, because they're strong veggies that can stand up to me and my grill. The bell peppers and asparagus, on the other hand, have to be handled carefully, so only flip them once. One of the more surprising things I've grilled is bread. Now, folks, don't try it with any little-ass, thin bread. You want crusty, rustic French bread for this recipe. The salad is packed with a boatload of different ingredients, from shallots and green onions to extra-sharp cheddar. We like cheddar for its salty, sharp flavor, but if you really wanted to play up the smokiness of the dish, you could use a smoked cheddar or Gouda.

---

2 zucchini, sliced horizontally into ⅓-inch pieces

1 yellow squash, sliced horizontally into ⅓-inch pieces

1 red bell pepper, seeded and cut into quarters

½ bunch asparagus (about 8 ounces)

6 ounces rustic French bread, cut into 1½-inch cubes

5 tablespoons olive oil, divided

Kosher salt and freshly ground black pepper

Juice of ½ lemon

Pinch of red-pepper flakes

8 ounces extra-sharp cheddar cheese, finely diced

3 green onions, sliced

1 cup grape tomatoes, sliced in half

1 small shallot, thinly sliced

1 large handful baby spinach

Heat grill to medium high.

Place the zucchini, yellow squash, bell pepper, asparagus, and cubed bread on a sheet tray, and drizzle with 3 tablespoons olive oil, and sprinkle with salt and pepper.

Arrange the cubed bread on the hot grill. Cook for 1½ minutes, or until slightly charred. Flip over, and cook for 1 minute more. Move croutons to the top grill shelf to continue toasting while you grill the vegetables. Grill veggies, flipping once, until slightly charred, about 6 minutes for squash, 10 minutes for pepper, and 8 minutes for asparagus. Let cool to just warm, then chop veggies into bite-sized pieces.

In a small bowl, whisk together the lemon juice and red-pepper flakes until smooth. Drizzle in the remaining 2 tablespoons olive oil, and whisk until emulsified. Season the dressing with a pinch of salt and pepper.

In a large bowl, combine the charred vegetables, croutons, cheddar, green onions, tomatoes, shallot, and handful of spinach. Toss everything together with the dressing.

Serves 6 to 8

Roasted Fingerling Potatoes with Fresh Herbs

Pat My girls always tease that my large fingers look like fingerling potatoes. I inherited my hands from my father and grandfather, and as I've cooked more over the years, I've grown to appreciate them as great tools for mixing up big bowls of ingredients and grabbing large handfuls of potatoes. My large hands (ring size is 15) are also great for hugging someone—just ask my girls. Roasting the potatoes in this recipe is super-easy, and each bite is filled with incredible crunch. Allow the olive oil and the fresh herbs to work together, put the potatoes on a baking sheet and into the oven, and this dish is done.

---

2 pounds fingerling potatoes,
   scrubbed well

6 cloves garlic

3 tablespoons olive oil

Kosher salt and freshly ground
   black pepper

1 tablespoon chopped fresh parsley

1 tablespoon chopped fresh dill

Preheat oven to 375 degrees F.

Place the potatoes and garlic on a rimmed sheet tray. Drizzle with olive oil, season with salt and pepper, and toss together. Roast for 25 minutes, until tender. Toss with chopped parsley and dill before serving.

Serves 4 to 6

Spicy Tomato Stewed Greens

Gina Many people aren't sure how to cook collard greens. In the South, they're often boiled to death with ham hocks, or just avoided altogether in favor of mustard and turnip greens. I've always loved collards, and I'm constantly trying to find new ways to prepare them. These stewed greens are incredible, and this dish has helped me make a collard fan out of a few nonbelievers. You won't miss the smoked ham hocks, turkey, or salt pork. I promise.

2 tablespoons olive oil
3 cloves garlic, chopped
1 teaspoon red-pepper flakes
2 pounds greens, stems discarded and
    leaves torn (mix of turnip, mustard,
    and collards—and any other green
    that catches your fancy)

One 14.5-ounce can diced tomatoes
2½ cups homemade or low-sodium
    store-bought chicken broth
2 teaspoons apple-cider vinegar
1 teaspoon sugar
Kosher salt and freshly ground
    black pepper, optional

Heat the olive oil in a large Dutch oven over medium-high heat. Add the garlic and red-pepper flakes, and sauté until garlic is fragrant, about 1 minute. Toss in the greens, tomatoes, chicken broth, vinegar, and sugar. Bring to a simmer, and cook for 20 minutes, until greens are tender. Taste, and season as necessary.

Serves 4 to 6

Black-Eyed Pea Cakes

Gina I remember fighting my mom about black-eyed peas when I was younger. I used to always complain, "Mom! These peas need work!" and she would reply, "Work 'em in your mouth!" After writing this recipe, I took a plate of black-eyed pea cakes over to her house to get her opinion before including it in this book. She tasted them and cried, "Look at my baby, all grown up!" You can't imagine how it made me feel to have her on board. When cooking these, rinse the peas first, before mashing them with the back of a spoon. Combine the flour and egg with the peas in a bowl, as for a traditional cake, but instead of baking, pan-fry the patty cakes instead. How about that?

2 strips bacon, finely chopped
1 small red onion, chopped
1 small jalapeño, ribs and seeds
    discarded, chopped
3 cloves garlic, chopped
Two 15-ounce cans black-eyed peas,
    drained and rinsed

⅓ cup all-purpose flour, plus more
    for dusting your hands
1 large egg, lightly beaten
3 tablespoons olive oil

Heat the bacon in a medium-sized heavy saucepan over medium heat. Cook, stirring, until some of its fat has rendered, about 3 minutes. Add the onion and jalapeño, and sauté until tender, about 4 minutes. Add the garlic, and sauté for the final minute. Turn off the heat, and stir in the drained beans. Mash with the back of a wooden spoon until most of the beans are mashed and everything is starting to stick and meld together. Spoon mashed beans into a bowl, stir in the flour and egg, and shape into eight ¼-cup patties.

Add oil to a large cast-iron skillet over medium heat. Once it's hot, place patties in the bottom of the skillet, and cook until brown and crisp on both sides, about 6 minutes total.

Serves 4 to 6

Cheesy Double Stuffed Potatoes

Pat We like a little smoke, in case you didn't know, so this is not your ordinary cheese potato. Instead of cheddar cheese, we use a creamy combination of Gouda, Parmesan, and sour cream. This dish is easy, and your oven will do most of the work. Just remember to keep it running once the potatoes are cooked, 'cause we are going to pop those babies back in. This side dish probably doesn't require a meat main course—although, if you wanted to add a juicy rib-eye to your menu, I wouldn't be mad at you.

---

4 large russet potatoes, well scrubbed (about 12 ounces each)

1 tablespoon olive oil

Kosher salt and freshly ground black pepper

2 tablespoons unsalted butter, sliced into pats

2 tablespoons grated Parmesan cheese

2 ounces cream cheese, at room temperature

½ cup sour cream

1 cup shredded smoked Gouda cheese

Preheat oven to 400 degrees F.

Prick the potatoes with a fork, drizzle with olive oil, and season with salt and pepper. Place directly on a rack in the center of the oven, and bake for 1 hour.

Remove the potatoes from the oven, and let them sit until cool enough to handle. Cut each potato in half lengthwise. Scoop out flesh into a large bowl. Discard four half-potato shells (we like to really fill up our potatoes!). Add butter, Parmesan, cream cheese, sour cream, and salt and pepper to the potato flesh. Using a hand mixer, beat the mixture until smooth and creamy. Add the Gouda in handfuls, and continue beating until it's incorporated. Refill the remaining 4 half-potato shells with the filling. Place the potatoes on a baking sheet, and put them back in the oven for another 30 minutes.

Serves 4

Summer Green Bean and Barley Salad

Gina Green beans are one of my favorite vegetables to eat in the summertime. They remind me of helping my grandmother prepare dinner. We used to sit on the back porch, me at her feet, and snap the ends off the beans together. She used to serve her green beans as a side dish, but the barley in this recipe makes the salad hearty enough to stand on its own as a meal.

Kosher salt, for the pot
1 pound green beans, ends trimmed,
  cut into 1-inch pieces
1 cup pearled barley
1 cup grape tomatoes,
  sliced in half
2 large handfuls baby mixed
  greens

CREAMY RED-WINE VINAIGRETTE
1 small shallot, finely chopped
1 tablespoon Dijon mustard
1 tablespoon mayonnaise
2 tablespoons red-wine vinegar
2 tablespoons olive oil
Kosher salt and freshly ground
  black pepper

In a large pot of salted boiling water, cook the beans until they're crisp, about 3 minutes. Remove the beans from the water with a spider (we'll use that water to cook the barley, too), and rinse in a colander under cold water to stop the cooking. Drain well, and put in a large bowl.

Add the barley to the same pot of boiling water, and cook for 45 minutes, or until tender. Drain well, and cool.

Mix the barley, tomatoes, greens, and green beans in a large bowl.

In a small bowl, whisk together the shallot, mustard, mayonnaise, and vinegar until combined. Drizzle in the olive oil, and whisk until emulsified. Season to taste with salt and pepper. Pour the dressing over the salad, toss well, and serve.

Serves 4 to 6

Shake It Up Salad with Basil Buttermilk Dressing

Gina I call this my "First Lady Salad," because we created it for the Easter Egg Roll at the White House. Mrs. Obama is all about her garden—which, let me tell you, is spectacular and huge. It brought back so many memories of our own family's backyard gardens that it took the formality out of our visit to the White House. I felt like I was just visiting a friend's house. I really support Mrs. Obama's farm-to-table movement and initiative to get Americans moving, so this recipe was a tribute to her. You can make the salad with any combination of your favorite ingredients, and we picked what we needed right from the garden. The shake-it-up part comes when you make the buttermilk dressing in a "Southern jug," as I call it (a Mason jar). Make sure you cover the lid tightly and shake vigorously, until it's all mixed together. Top the salad with dressing, and toss well with tongs. As the First Lady says, shake it up and get moving!

---

1 head green-leaf lettuce, chopped
2 carrots, peeled and shredded
4 radishes, sliced
1 cup cherry tomatoes, sliced in half

BASIL BUTTERMILK DRESSING
¼ cup low-fat buttermilk
¼ cup sour cream
¼ cup loosely packed fresh basil, chopped
Kosher salt and freshly ground black pepper

In a large bowl, combine the lettuce, carrots, radishes, and cherry tomatoes.

Put the buttermilk, sour cream, basil, and salt and pepper in a Mason jar. Screw on the lid tightly, and shake vigorously until all mixed together.

Top the salad with dressing, and toss well with tongs.

Serves 6

Kale Salad with Chopped Almonds, Feta, and Champagne Vinaigrette

Gina I love kale—sautéed or baked in the oven, it doesn't matter. I used to have a tough time finding it (I'd have to ask the produce guy if he had any in the back), but now that it's popular, you can find it in most grocery stores. People don't look at me funny in the check-out line when I'm buying it anymore, but I'm not convinced that they're much more excited about eating it. I'm betting this recipe just might change their minds.

I don't care for the tough stems, so I tear the leaves off. Kale can be a tad bitter, but adding the sweet Gala apple helps balance out the flavors. The almonds provide a nice crunchy texture, and the crumbled feta cheese and champagne-vinaigrette dressing give the salad a creamy finish. Yes, ma'am, I know you are thinking I love the champagne part, and you are correct.

---

1 bunch curly kale (about 8 ounces),
  stemmed and chopped
1 Gala apple, diced
⅓ cup roasted salted almonds, chopped
¼ red onion, thinly sliced
½ cup crumbled feta cheese

CHAMPAGNE VINAIGRETTE
1 tablespoon honey
2 tablespoons champagne vinegar
¼ cup olive oil
Kosher salt and freshly ground
  black pepper

In a large bowl, combine the kale with the apple, almonds, and onion.

In a small bowl, whisk together the honey and vinegar until combined. Drizzle in the olive oil, and whisk until emulsified. Season with salt and pepper. Pour the dressing over the kale, and toss well for 2 minutes. Sprinkle in the feta, and toss again. Cover with plastic wrap, and let sit out at room temperature for at least 30 minutes, so the kale will soften.

Serves 4 to 6

Tip This salad can be made up to a day ahead of time, since the kale will soften as it sits in the dressing and absorb more flavor. If you prefer a crisper salad, serve immediately.

Not Your Basic Sweet Potato Salad

Gina I love this potato salad, because it's a nice alternative to the traditional mayo-laden potato salad made with russet and red potatoes. The sweet potatoes go well with the smokiness of the bacon, the sweet-and-tart flavors of orange juice and marmalade, and the spicy flavors of the chipotle pepper in adobo sauce. Add the dressing to the potatoes while they're still warm, so that the flavors can all soak in together.

---

3 medium sweet potatoes (about 2 pounds), peeled and cut into 1-inch cubes
Kosher salt and freshly ground black pepper
2 stalks celery, chopped
½ small red onion, finely chopped

5 strips bacon, cooked and crumbled
¾ cup mayonnaise
2 tablespoons orange juice
1 tablespoon orange marmalade
1 canned chipotle pepper, minced, plus 1 teaspoon adobo sauce from can

---

Add the sweet potatoes to a large pot of cold salted water. Bring to a boil over medium-high heat. Reduce to a simmer, and cook until tender, about 12 minutes. Drain the potatoes well, and while they're still warm, add them to a large bowl with the celery, onion, and bacon.

In a medium bowl, while potatoes are cooking, whisk together the mayonnaise, orange juice, orange marmalade, chipotle pepper, and adobo sauce until smooth. Pour the dressing over potatoes while they're still warm, and toss well together. Cover the salad with plastic wrap, and chill for at least 1 hour before serving.

Serves 6

Vinegar Slaw

Pat Gina and I love to play around with different ingredients for our slaw recipes. When we visited North Carolina several years ago, we tasted a vinegar-based slaw and BBQ that blew us away. Mind you, I was never a big fan of too much apple-cider vinegar, and in Carolina they use it as liberally as we drink sweet tea in Memphis, but, damn, that slaw was good! (There's a rivalry over who has the best 'cue, so that last statement might get me in trouble in Memphis.)

---

1 small head green cabbage (about 2 pounds), shredded
½ large red onion, grated
2 large carrots, peeled and grated
2 tablespoons yellow mustard
2 tablespoons sugar

⅔ cup apple-cider vinegar
½ cup vegetable oil
1 teaspoon celery seeds
Pinch of cayenne pepper
Kosher salt and freshly ground black pepper

In your largest bowl, combine the cabbage, red onion, and carrots together, and give it a toss.

Whisk together the mustard, sugar, vinegar, vegetable oil, celery seeds, cayenne, and salt and pepper until emulsified. Pour over the coleslaw, and toss well again. Cover with plastic wrap, and chill for at least 2 hours before serving.

Serves 8

Tip For color, try to use as much of the outer, dark-green leaves of the cabbage as possible. The sugar and cayenne will balance the apple-cider vinegar, giving you a delicious tangy, sweet coleslaw. We love it as a side, or piled high on any BBQ dish.

Grilled Steak Salad with Bacon and Blue Cheese

Pat This hearty dish is the salad version of a traditional steak dinner. In place of a wedge of iceberg lettuce and a side of baked potato, we combine green beans, butter lettuce, and boiled new potatoes as the base of the dish. Then we add steakhouse seasonings with crumbled blue cheese, chives, and our favorite pig (bacon). While Gina whips up the vinaigrette, I man the grill. When you pull the flank steak off the heat, remember to let it sit for a few minutes before slicing. Cut the steak against the grain. Toss your salad, and lay the slices of steak across the top. Now, don't that sound yummy?

Kosher salt and freshly ground
  black pepper
8 ounces green beans, trimmed and
  cut into bite-sized pieces
8 ounces small red potatoes, quartered
1 large head butter lettuce, leaves torn
1 cup cherry tomatoes, sliced in half
¼ cup finely chopped red onion

¼ cup sliced fresh chives
2 ounces blue cheese, crumbled
4 strips bacon, cooked and crumbled
1 clove garlic, minced
2 tablespoons red-wine vinegar
¼ cup olive oil
1 pound flank steak, trimmed
  of visible fat

Heat grill to medium-high heat.

Bring a large saucepan of salted water up to a boil. Cook the green beans in the water for 3 minutes, or until tender. Remove to a colander and rinse under cold water to stop the cooking.

Add potatoes to a medium pot of cold salted water and bring to a boil. Reduce to a simmer, and cook for 10 to 12 minutes, or until tender. Drain and let cool.

Combine the green beans, potatoes, lettuce, tomatoes, onion, chives, blue cheese, and bacon in a bowl. Whisk together the garlic and vinegar in a small bowl. Whisk in the olive oil until smooth, and season with salt and pepper.

Sprinkle the steak well with salt and pepper. Grill for 4 to 5 minutes on each side, for medium. Let rest at least 5 minutes before slicing across the grain into ½-inch-thick slices.

Toss the salad with the vinaigrette, then lay the steak slices on top.

Serves 4 as a main course

Broccoli Slaw

Gina I can't stand a soggy, limp slaw; I need some crunch and bite! Spenser and Shelbi are huge fans of broccoli, so I started experimenting with broccoli slaw and found it was something that suited all of our tastes. Pat and I added dried cranberries for a little sweetness, sunflower seeds for a little saltiness, and a Greek-yogurt-based dressing for a little tanginess. You know I had to add a little extra of me in there, too; hence the cayenne pepper (which we totally argued—I mean, debated—about including). There you have it—some damn fine crunchy slaw.

One 12-ounce package broccoli-slaw mix
¼ small red onion, thinly sliced
2 stalks celery, sliced
½ cup dried cranberries
½ cup roasted and salted sunflower seeds
⅓ cup reduced-fat Greek yogurt

⅓ cup reduced-fat mayonnaise
2 tablespoons apple-cider vinegar
Dash of cayenne pepper
1 teaspoon sugar
Kosher salt and freshly ground black pepper

Pour the slaw mix into a large bowl. Toss in the onion, celery, cranberries, and sunflower seeds. In a separate, small bowl, whisk together the yogurt, mayonnaise, cider vinegar, cayenne, sugar, and salt and pepper. The dressing will be thick from the yogurt. Add the dressing to the slaw, and mix very well. Serve right away for maximum crunch, or cover with plastic wrap and chill before serving.

Serves 4 to 6

THE GADGETLESS KITCHEN

Pat My grandparents didn't rely on many of the gadgets or tools common in our kitchens today. For example, instead of tongs, they used large spoons and forks. In fact, Daddy Milton made his own BBQ fork by taking two pieces of metal and sharpening them to points, then attaching them to an 18-inch piece of wood. And my grandparents had just one knife in their kitchen, a big wood-handled thing. This knife was always off limits to me; I remember my grandfather had a large piece of stone he used to keep it razor-sharp. It just goes to show, a cook can never blame his tools: good food is all about the love and technique that goes into it.

Picnic Rice Salad

Gina When I was little, I called this the "crunchy dish," and whenever I think about it now, I can see my mom racing to prepare for a family summer picnic. I was the youngest, so I didn't get to help out too much, but my older siblings would help her by chopping veggies. My sister and I would entertain everyone by doing a dance we called "the bump," and our siblings would occasionally toss chopped pieces of veggies— the tomatoes, cucumbers, and celery—across the room to see if we could catch them in our mouths. This salad brings back so many good memories of my family laughing and spending time together, and I hope it brings laughter to your family, too.

1½ cups long-grain white rice

1 red bell pepper, seeded and chopped

1 medium English cucumber, diced

One 10.5-ounce container grape tomatoes, sliced in half

½ small red onion, finely chopped

2 stalks celery, chopped

2 tablespoons roughly chopped fresh basil

2 tablespoons roughly chopped fresh parsley

3 green onions, sliced

½ cup roughly chopped walnuts

Grated zest and juice of 1 lime

3 tablespoons rice-wine vinegar

⅓ cup canola oil

2 tablespoons light-brown sugar

Kosher salt and freshly ground black pepper

Cook the rice in a large saucepan as directed on packaging. Let cool, and fluff with a fork.

Put the rice in a large bowl. Toss in the bell pepper, cucumber, grape tomatoes, red onion, celery, herbs, green onions, and walnuts.

Prepare the dressing in a small bowl: whisk together the lime zest and juice, vinegar, canola oil, and light-brown sugar, and season with a big pinch of salt and pepper.

Drizzle the salad with the dressing, and toss to combine. Taste, and adjust seasoning if necessary.

Serves 6 to 8

Meats

Country Fried Steak with Black Pepper and Cream Gravy

Tangy, Sweet and Sour Pot Roast

Old School Braised Oxtails

Low and Slow Pulled Pork

Oven-Roasted Ribs (AKA Apartment Ribs)

Smoky Chicken and Rice Skillet

Hot Honey Peach Chicken

Skillet Roasted Chicken

Weekday Not Fried Chicken

Sunday Fried Chicken with Red Hot Maple Glaze

Blackened Catfish with Creole Rémoulade

Halibut with Kale and Mushrooms

Smoked Sausage Shrimp and Grits

Pat Meat has always been the centerpiece of our table. Hearty recipes that remind us of our grandparents like Tangy, Sweet and Sour Pot Roast and Oven-Roasted Ribs may bring you back to your childhood, too. I had to include a pork recipe (of course), and I'll show you a new way to slow-cook pork using your Dutch oven. You can make the entire thing from your kitchen—no smoking or grilling needed.

Even when it comes to other forms of cooking, the important thing to remember about meat is that you're not actively cooking it the entire time—all you have to do is prep, and then the oven takes over. Seasoning meat can also always be done the day before, and I am a big fan of how much more flavor this gives the meat. If you don't take the time to marinate properly, you run the risk of having your dish come out bland, so sit that meat in the seasoning and let all the flavors get to know each other overnight! When it comes to dinner the next night, all you have to do is follow instructions and the meal will cook itself.

Country Fried Steak with Black Pepper and Cream Gravy

Gina This dish takes me back to the good ole days of sitting around the dinner table with my sisters. We'd talk about our day over a big country-fried steak dinner. To make this meal, my mom would go to the local butcher, chat with him for a while to put him in a good mood, then tell him that she needed the most tender cube steak he had. She'd get him to check all the meat, to make sure she was buying the best pieces. Twenty years later, I now find myself going through the same grocery-store routine when I want to cook this for my family. I serve it just as Mom did, with garlic mashed potatoes and green beans. I think all that is missing is the cherry-flavored Kool-Aid!

---

2 cups all-purpose flour

1 teaspoon garlic powder

1 teaspoon paprika

¼ teaspoon cayenne pepper

Kosher salt and freshly ground
   black pepper

3 eggs, well beaten

¾ cup low-fat buttermilk

2 dashes of hot sauce, divided

2 pounds cube steaks

⅓ cup vegetable oil, plus more if needed

2 cups whole milk

3 green onions, sliced, for garnish

Put the flour, garlic powder, paprika, cayenne, and a big pinch of salt and pepper in a pie plate, and whisk together until well combined. Put the eggs, buttermilk, and a dash of hot sauce in a second pie plate, and whisk well together.

Slice the cube steaks into manageable pieces if they are larger than your hand. Season steaks well with salt and pepper.

Preheat oven to 200 degrees F.

Heat the oil in a large cast-iron skillet over medium-high heat. It's very important for the oil to be hot enough, or you will end up with a soggy, oil-soaked steak (see Tip for testing heat).

Working one piece of meat at a time, dredge the steak first through the flour mixture, then the eggs, letting excess drip off. Then dredge it back through the flour, and place it in the hot skillet. Add up to three steaks (being careful not to overcrowd your skillet, or the oil temperature will drop) to the hot oil, and fry until golden brown, 4 to 5 minutes per side. Remove to a wire-rack-lined baking sheet, and keep in the oven while you finish the next batch. Continue dredging the next batch of steaks once the steaks before them come out of the skillet. If needed, add more oil to the skillet in between batches.

continued on next page

continued from previous page

Pour off all but 3 tablespoons of the oil from the skillet, and remove any badly burned bits. Sprinkle 3 tablespoons of the seasoned flour into the skillet. Cook, whisking, until the flour is golden, about 2 minutes. Slowly whisk in the milk. Bring to a boil, then reduce to a simmer and cook for about 5 minutes, or until the gravy is thick. If the gravy becomes too thick, you can thin out with water or more milk. Stir in 1 teaspoon of the black pepper and a dash of hot sauce, and taste for seasoning. Add more salt and pepper if necessary. Plate the steaks drizzled with gravy, and sprinkled with sliced green onions.

Serves 4

Tip for Frying When heating your oil for frying, test the heat by throwing a pinch of flour into the oil. If it spits, it means the oil is hot enough.

Tangy, Sweet and Sour Pot Roast

Pat Some of my fondest memories of growing up took place during football season, in the fall. From first grade until my second year of college, I always spent the hot Memphis summers working and training for the upcoming fall season. My older brothers used to tell me, "If you stay in shape during the summer, practice won't be as hard once the season starts." I ran sprints, lifted weights, cut drills, and did everything else I could to get in tip-top shape. I was always starving after a long day of practicing, and one of my favorite dinner meals to come home to during football season was my mom's pot roast. It was hearty, warm, and one of those few meals that always yielded seconds. My mom worked from 8:00 to 5:00 during the day, so she relied on her Dutch oven to do most of the work for her. She'd season one big ole chuck roast the night before, and then the next morning, before she headed out to work, she would put it in the oven to slow cook all day. When she got home that evening, she would add what she called fillers—carrots, potatoes, peas, corn, and anything else she could think of—to increase servings.

Brown the roast on all sides first, to ensure even cooking; then the Dutch oven cooks it until it's as tender as a baby's butt. We use the juices from this roast to sauté our garlic and onions. Gina and I don't have any boys playing football in our house, so we don't need as many fillers in our version of Mama's pot roast, and we always throw in some of our favorite fingerling potatoes. This roast brings me right back to my glory days.

---

3 pounds chuck roast
Kosher salt and freshly ground
  black pepper
2 tablespoons olive oil
2 onions, cut into thin wedges
5 cloves garlic, smashed and peeled
1 dried bay leaf
½ cup red-wine vinegar

½ cup tomato juice
3 cups homemade or low-sodium
  store-bought chicken broth
1 tablespoon brown sugar
1 tablespoon Creole mustard
1 tablespoon Worcestershire sauce
1 pound fingerling potatoes

Preheat oven to 350 degrees F. Adjust your oven racks to accommodate a 5-quart Dutch oven or some other large, oven-safe pot with a tight-fitting lid.

Season the roast with salt and pepper. Heat the oil in the Dutch oven over medium-high heat. Once it's simmering, place the roast in the pan and brown on both sides for 4 to 5 minutes. Remove to a large plate. Add the onions, garlic, and bay leaf to the pot, and cook until onions are very tender and lightly golden, about 8 minutes. Stir in the red-

continued on next page

continued from previous page

wine vinegar, tomato juice, chicken broth, brown sugar, mustard, and Worcestershire sauce. Bring the liquid to a boil, and put the roast and any accumulated juices back in the pot. Cover with a lid, and place in the oven. Cook for 2 hours. Check to make sure the liquid still comes halfway up the roast; if not, add water. Flip the roast. Add the potatoes, and return the roast to the oven. Cook for 1 hour and 15 minutes more, or until fork-tender.

Remove the roast to a cutting board, and put the potatoes in a bowl, making sure to remove the bay leaf. Loosely tent both with foil. Place the Dutch oven on the stove, over medium-high heat, and simmer for 5 minutes, until the sauce is thick. Slice the roast against the grain into ½-inch slices. Serve meat and potatoes ladled with sauce.

Serves 6 to 8

Old School Braised Oxtails

Gina Mama Callie used to make oxtails all the time, but since they were expensive, she'd prepare a different type of meat for us and push her oxtails to the back of the stove. I remember asking her about it one day.

"What's that?"

"What?" she said.

"That funny-looking meat."

"Oh," she replied, "I'm just making a little soup."

This was a lie, of course (she liked to keep them for herself), but I didn't know it at the time. Oxtails were often used in soups, because you could stretch the meat a lot further. They're easier to get these days, and I serve them to my girls over hot buttered rice. Since they look like, well, oxtails, it took me a while to get Spenser and Shelbi to try them. I eventually told them to close their eyes and let their tongues do the judging—and I won every time.

Oxtails remind me just how much I miss my great-grandmother, and how sad it is that she didn't get the chance to see my girls grow up or get to know me as an adult. But they also remind me how she used to cook with all the love in the world, putting hours of work into a dish just because she knew it would make her family happy. Food was her gift to us, and I try to give my family the same love from my own kitchen.

3½ pounds oxtails, cut into 2-inch-thick
  pieces
Kosher salt and freshly ground
  black pepper
½ cup all-purpose flour
2 tablespoons vegetable oil
1 Vidalia onion, chopped
5 cloves garlic, smashed and peeled
1 cup red wine
3 cups homemade or low-sodium
  store-bought chicken broth

3 tablespoons tomato paste
Dash of Worcestershire
  sauce
1 dried bay leaf
1 pound russet potatoes, peeled
  and cubed
3 large carrots, scrubbed and cut into
  2-inch chunks (unpeeled)
Hot buttered rice, for serving

Preheat oven to 325 degrees F.

Heat a large Dutch oven over medium-high heat. Season the oxtails on all sides with a big pinch of salt and pepper. Put the flour on a pie plate, and whisk in another pinch of salt and pepper. Dredge the oxtails through the flour, dusting off excess.

continued on next page

continued from previous page

Add oil to the Dutch oven, and when it's hot, brown oxtails on both sides, 8 to 10 minutes total. Remove to a plate, and drain off some of the grease if necessary. Add the onion and garlic, and sauté until tender, about 5 minutes.

Pour in the wine, scraping up any browned bits that may be stuck on the bottom of the pan. Let the wine reduce for a few minutes. Stir in the broth, tomato paste, Worcestershire sauce, and bay leaf, and bring to a boil. Reduce heat, add the browned oxtails and any juices that may be on the plate, and cover with a lid.

Place in oven, and cook for 4 hours, checking occasionally to make sure the liquid hasn't reduced below the halfway mark, and add water if needed. Add the potatoes and carrots for the last hour of cooking. You may need to nestle them gently in between the oxtails, to make sure they are submerged in the cooking liquid. Skim off any visible fat floating on the surface, remove the bay leaf, and serve over hot buttered rice.

Serves 4 to 6

"MAMA CALLIE" CLARK

Gina My relationship with Mama Callie is where my love of cooking came from. When I was growing up, she was always in the kitchen, seven days a week, preparing some love for us that may not have been as easily communicated as it was shown. I was the youngest in the house and her favorite. (My sisters will tell you a different story, but since this is my book, I only have to give my opinion.) Mama Callie used to let me hang out in the kitchen with her, which I loved. From Braised Oxtails to Fried Apple Hand Pies, that little lady could "throw down" in the kitchen. She was more than just a great cook; she taught me many invaluable lessons that I apply to my life on a daily basis.

She was considered the head of our family, and everyone gathered at her house after church on Sunday. Her house was only a block away from the church, which was convenient, since she didn't drive. She was a devout Christian, and if you stayed with her on Saturday night, your butt was in church on Sunday morning.

Mama Callie's home was open to everyone, and there was nothing she liked better than seeing family and friends spending time together over a good meal. She strongly believed that cooking does for the soul what a doctor does for a sick patient. Goodness, I miss her.

Low and Slow Pulled Pork

Pat Y'all know Gina isn't a fan of manning an outdoor grill or a smoker. She loves BBQ as much as I do, but she doesn't like getting all the charcoal and hickory smoke into her hair. That's not a problem for me, because, if you haven't noticed, I don't have any hair. Of course, that's not the only reason we love this delicious oven-cooked dish. It's great for the winter, when my grill is packed up for the season.

There are several key steps to keep in mind. First: *low* and *slow*! This means cook slowly, at a low temperature for several hours. You don't have to sit on the patio for hours, watching it cook over an open charcoal-and-hickory wood fire, but you do have to do a little preparation and rub your butt the night before. (Y'all keep it clean; I'm talking about the Boston pork butt.) Using our basic dry-rub ingredients—paprika, cayenne, cumin, mustard powder, and celery seeds—massage the spices into the meat, cover with foil, and let it sit in the fridge overnight.

It gets really easy from there. Just put the pork in the oven for several hours and it will cook itself. Pulled pork means it should pull apart once it's done. If you can't pull it apart easily with your hands, it ain't done! Once it's fully cooked, you have two textures to enjoy: the browned, flavorful, crusty meat on the outside, and the moist, tender white meat inside. Add a huge amount of this pulled pork to a very soft bun with coleslaw and our fantastic BBQ sauce and you've got what we sometimes refer to as a jumbo. (It's a Southern term used in a lot of BBQ restaurants for a very large BBQ sandwich. Some of them can have a total weight of up to a pound!)

½ cup sugar

¼ cup kosher salt

1 tablespoon smoked paprika

1 tablespoon cayenne pepper

2 teaspoons ground cumin

½ teaspoon ground celery seed

½ teaspoon mustard powder

8½-pound bone-in Boston butt

10 to 12 soft hamburger buns

BBQ Sauce (recipe follows)

Vinegar Slaw (page 82)

To make the dry rub, whisk together the sugar, salt, paprika, cayenne, cumin, celery seed, and mustard powder. Reserve 4 tablespoons, both for the BBQ sauce and for serving later on. Generously sprinkle all sides of the pork butt with the remaining rub, making sure to get some seasoning into all the crevices, and massage the seasoning into the meat. Cover with plastic wrap, and refrigerate for at least 4 hours or up to 1 day in advance.

Preheat oven to 275 degrees F. Line a roasting pan with heavy-duty foil.

continued on page 99

continued from page 97

Place the pork in the roasting pan, fat side up, and cook the meat until extremely tender, about 8 hours. The meat will have shrunk up a bit, and the exterior will be nice and dark. The meat will easily twist when you insert a fork into it.

Once the pork is tender, remove from the oven and let rest until it's cool enough to handle, about 20 minutes. Using 2 forks, shred the pork into bite-sized pieces right in the roasting pan, so it will absorb all the flavorful juices from the bottom of the pan.

Pile some pork on the bottom of each bun, paint with some BBQ sauce, top with slaw, and close with the top of the bun. Serve with extra rub and sauce on the side.

Serves 10 to 12

BBQ Sauce

1½ cups ketchup

½ cup apple-cider vinegar

3 tablespoons sugar

1 tablespoon Worcestershire sauce

1½ teaspoons garlic powder

1 teaspoon paprika

1 teaspoon cayenne pepper

½ teaspoon liquid smoke

Combine all the ingredients in a saucepan, and simmer over medium-low heat for 10 minutes. Sauce can be stored up to 2 weeks in a tightly sealed refrigerated container.

Makes 2 cups

Oven-Roasted Ribs
(AKA Apartment Ribs)

Pat Over twenty years ago, before Gina and I were married, we didn't have the luxury of a big backyard and all the BBQ equipment we have today. We lived in a tiny one-bedroom apartment and didn't have a patio or balcony to grill on. There was a single oven, in a kitchen so small everything was within arm's reach. This forced us to get pretty darn creative with our cooking methods, and we eventually figured out a way to make ribs without a grill. Just season the rack of ribs with our dry rub overnight or for several hours, and cook it in the oven, tightly covered with a sheet of foil. Baste the rack with BBQ sauce for the last 15 minutes of the cooking process, and get ready for finger-lickin' good ribs.

2 tablespoons kosher salt

2 tablespoons light-brown sugar

2 tablespoons paprika

1 teaspoon cayenne pepper

1 teaspoon ground cumin

1 teaspoon smoked paprika

2 racks baby back ribs (about 2 to 2½ pounds each rack)

BBQ Sauce (see preceding recipe)

Whisk all the ingredients except ribs and BBQ Sauce together in a small bowl.

Pat the ribs dry with paper towels, and place them, curl side up, on a flat work surface. Using your fingers, pull off the thick white membrane on the underside of the ribs. This will allow the flavors of the rub to permeate the meat fully. Place the ribs on a rimmed sheet tray, and season all sides with the spice rub. Cover with plastic wrap, and refrigerate for at least 2 hours, or up to 1 day in advance.

Preheat oven to 325 degrees F.

Place the ribs in a roasting pan, meat side up, and cover tightly with foil. Roast for 1 hour and 30 minutes.

Turn up heat to 450 degrees F. Generously baste ribs with BBQ sauce on both sides. Place back in oven and roast for 15 minutes more, or until the outsides of the ribs are nicely browned in spots and glazed well with the sauce. Slice between the bones into individual ribs. Serve with extra sauce on the side.

Serves 4

Smoky Chicken and Rice Skillet

Gina This is my one-pot specialty. You can use any part of the chicken in this dish, but I'm partial to thighs because of their rich flavor and tender meat. (I use thighs for most recipes that call for chicken parts.) Since everything is seasoned and cooked in the same skillet, the chicken, sausage, and veggies all borrow flavors from one another. This dish is easy to make, really filling, and great for leftovers. And there's only one dish to clean!

---

4 chicken thighs, skinless and boneless
   (about 1¼ pounds)
Kosher salt and freshly ground
   black pepper
2 tablespoons olive oil
6 ounces smoked sausage
   (such as kielbasa)
1 red onion, chopped
1 red bell pepper, seeded and chopped

3 cloves garlic, minced
1 teaspoon smoked paprika
1½ cups long-grain white rice
One 14.5-ounce can diced tomatoes,
   juice drained
3½ cups homemade or low-sodium
   store-bought chicken broth
1 cup frozen peas

Heat a large high-sided skillet over medium-high heat. Season the chicken with salt and pepper. Add the olive oil to the skillet, and once it's hot, sauté the sausage until brown, 4 to 6 minutes. Remove sausage from pan. Add chicken to the pan and brown on all sides, about 6 minutes. Remove chicken to a plate. Add the onion and bell pepper to the pan, and sauté until the pepper is tender, about 5 minutes. Add garlic for the last minute of cooking. Season with smoked paprika, salt, and pepper. Stir in the rice until it's coated well with the oil and seasonings. Add the can of tomatoes, the broth, the sausage, and the browned chicken pieces. Bring to a boil. Reduce heat to low, cover the pan, and cook until the chicken is cooked through, the rice is tender, and the liquid is absorbed, about 30 minutes. Sprinkle peas over the top of the rice for the last 3 minutes of cooking.

Serves 4

Tip If you're using a very large skillet, you may need to turn it 180 degrees halfway through cooking, so everything cooks evenly.

Hot Honey Peach Chicken

Gina My mom taught me every chicken dish she knew, so when I first started cooking for my family, I "chickened" them to death. Spenser used to complain, "I'm gonna grow feathers!" Pat and I were a young couple, and chicken was very affordable, so I tried to come up with new ways to serve it, so my girls wouldn't get tired of the same thing every night. This dish was a winner. The honey and peach nectar add a sweetness that balances out the spice of the chipotle chili powder and Dijon. The secret ingredient here is really the peach nectar. It adds a subtle, fresh peach flavor to the dish and gives the chicken a juicy glaze. Now it no longer looks like boring baked chicken . . . again!

⅓ cup honey
4 tablespoons salted butter, melted
¼ cup peach nectar
1 tablespoon Dijon mustard
1 teaspoon chipotle chili powder

Kosher salt and freshly ground
   black pepper
3½ pounds chicken pieces (breasts,
   thighs, drumsticks)

Preheat oven to 350 degrees F. Line a sheet tray with foil.

In a medium bowl, whisk the honey, melted butter, peach nectar, mustard, chipotle, and a pinch of salt and pepper until smooth.

Season the chicken on all sides with salt and pepper. Drizzle the sauce over the chicken pieces, and toss to coat well. Line the chicken up on the sheet tray making sure there is space between the pieces. Bake in the oven for 1 hour, until browned and cooked through. Baste with pan drippings halfway through cooking time. Remove from oven, and let the chicken rest for 10 minutes. Baste with the pan drippings until glossy and well coated.

Serves 4 to 6

Skillet Roasted Chicken

Gina Do you remember "Get Yo' Man Chicken" from our first cookbook, *Down Home with the Neelys*? Well, you could say this is "Keep Yo' Man Chicken." Mama Callie always said there are several ways to a man's heart and one is his stomach. Not only will he be at your command after eating this dish, but you'll be able to keep him around a few years longer because you're not serving him fried chicken. And, guys, I don't mean to leave you out: if you prepare this meal for your sweetie, she might just be extra special to you later.

If you don't have a cast-iron skillet, go buy one or go to Grandma's house and borrow hers. Nothing creates even, sustained heat like cast iron, and it cooks on the stovetop or in the oven equally well. Olive oil will help brown the chicken perfectly and lend a subtle flavor to the roasted carrot, parsnip, sweet potato, and shallots. Don't forget to season inside the cavity of your chicken with garlic, thyme, and rosemary. Once you pull this baby out of the oven, let it rest before you start carving. Trust me, whoever you're cooking for will be grinning from ear to ear.

One 5-pound chicken
Kosher salt and freshly ground
    black pepper
3 sprigs each fresh thyme and rosemary
2 cloves garlic, smashed and peeled
1 carrot, peeled and cut into 1-inch
    chunks

1 parsnip, peeled and cut into 1-inch
    chunks
1 sweet potato, peeled and cut into
    1-inch cubes
2 shallots, peeled (and sliced in half
    if large)
3 tablespoons olive oil, divided

Preheat oven to 475 degrees F.

Pat the chicken dry with paper towels. Season the inside of the cavity generously with salt and pepper, and stuff the sprigs of thyme and rosemary into the cavity, along with the garlic.

Toss the vegetables in a bowl with 2 tablespoons olive oil, salt, and pepper, until glossy and well coated. Place the vegetables in a single layer in the bottom of a 12-inch cast-iron skillet. Place chicken, breast side up, on top of the vegetables, and drizzle with the remaining tablespoon of olive oil. Lightly massage the oil into the skin, and season the chicken all over with salt and pepper.

Place the skillet in the center rack of the oven, and bake for 25 minutes. Lower the heat to 400 degrees F, and continue roasting for 1 hour, or until the chicken is thoroughly cooked and the juices run clear. Let the chicken rest for 15 minutes before carving. Serve with the roasted vegetables and pan juices.

Serves 4 to 6

Weekday Not Fried Chicken

Gina Is it really possible to have fried chicken and not fry it? You bet your sweet Gina it is. I have fooled so many people with this recipe. You just have to remember to keep your mouth closed until everyone tastes it.

The most important step is to let the chicken sit at room temperature as you prepare the other ingredients and get that oven good and hot. The Greek-yogurt-and-mustard base really helps the garlic powder and cayenne pepper stick to the chicken. Now the fun ingredient: cornflakes! They're what gives the chicken the texture and look of fried chicken. Just make sure to spritz the chicken with nonstick cooking spray as it cooks, to help brown and crisp up the coating. Then pour yourself a glass of wine to wait as you "fry" chicken. You might throw a little flour on your blouse, just for the sake of appearances.

Nonstick spray

One 3½-pound chicken, cut into
    10 pieces, backbone and wing tips
    removed

2 teaspoons kosher salt

1 teaspoon freshly ground black pepper

½ teaspoon garlic powder

1 cup low-fat Greek yogurt

1 tablespoon Creole mustard

1 tablespoon hot sauce

5 cups cornflakes

¼ teaspoon cayenne pepper

Preheat oven to 425 degrees F. Place a wire rack inside a rimmed sheet tray, and spritz lightly with the nonstick spray.

Season the chicken with the salt, pepper, and garlic powder. Let sit at room temperature while you prepare the other ingredients and the oven comes up to temperature.

In a pie plate, combine the yogurt, mustard, and hot sauce.

Put the cornflakes in a separate casserole dish, and crush them with your hands. Sprinkle in the cayenne, and whisk together to combine.

Dredge the seasoned chicken through the wet mixture, then through the cornflake mixture. Arrange on the prepared sheet tray, making sure there is ample space between the pieces of chicken. Give the chicken a spritz with the nonstick cooking spray. This will help brown and crisp the coating.

Bake for 45 to 50 minutes, until the chicken is crisp and cooked through.

Serves 4 to 6

Sunday Fried Chicken with Red Hot Maple Glaze

Pat Gina and I travel all over the country to give live cooking demonstrations for our fans. We always have microphones in the audience so we can talk to our guests, and they ask us all sorts of questions. One of the most memorable came from a young married woman, in her late twenties, from somewhere up north. She asked us how to fry chicken. This seemed like a trick question. Hell, our daughter Shelbi (who was about thirteen at the time) knew how to fry chicken. This woman wasn't joking, though. She had never fried chicken with much success. She said either she undercooked it, and even though it was golden and crispy on the outside it was still raw on the inside, or she overcooked it, and once it cooled it was brick-hard and just as dry on the inside. In light of that woman's question, I told Gina we shouldn't assume everyone knows how to fry chicken, and write a simple recipe that anyone can follow.

We like to season our chicken the night before, cover it in plastic wrap, and let it sit in the fridge until we're ready to cook. Great fried chicken is golden, with crispy outer skin and succulent moist meat on the inside. There are several key steps to great fried chicken. First, make sure your chicken is warmed to room temperature before cooking. This helps the chicken cook evenly and keeps the peanut oil at the right temperature. Second, dredge each piece through the wet mixture before the seasoned flour, so the flour sticks to the meat and creates a crispy crust when fried. And, third, make sure to not overcrowd your skillet. You have to give that chicken space to cook!

Now that you've made perfect fried chicken, turn it up a notch with our red hot maple glaze. Cook the glaze before you start frying your chicken so that it has plenty of time to reduce and thicken. We hope this helps that young lady in the audience. We're sure her husband will appreciate the recipe, too.

One 3½-pound chicken, cut into
   10 pieces, backbone and wing tips
   removed
2 teaspoons kosher salt
1 teaspoon freshly ground black pepper
1 teaspoon paprika
½ teaspoon garlic powder

Peanut oil, for frying
1½ cups low-fat buttermilk
2 large eggs, whisked
Dash of hot sauce
1¾ cups self-rising flour
Red Hot Maple Glaze (recipe follows)

Put the chicken in a casserole dish. Combine the salt, pepper, paprika, and garlic powder in a small bowl, reserving ½ teaspoon of the mixture. Sprinkle the remaining spice mixture on

continued on next page

continued from previous page

both sides of the chicken. Let sit in the seasonings in the fridge for at least 3 hours, or up to 1 day ahead.

Take the chicken out of the fridge to remove the chill a full hour before you fry.

Heat the oil in a fryer or large straight-sided cast-iron skillet to 350 degrees F. If using a skillet, do not fill more than halfway with oil.

Whisk together the buttermilk, eggs, and hot sauce in a pie plate.

Add the flour to a casserole dish, and season with the reserved spice mixture.

Working in batches, add the chicken to the buttermilk, shaking off excess, and place, a few pieces at a time, in the flour mixture to dredge.

Place the chicken in the hot oil, and fry until golden and crisp, about 10 minutes for white meat and 13 to 15 minutes for dark meat. Remove from the fryer to a wire rack (to keep it crispy), and cool for 10 minutes before serving. Serve chicken with the red hot maple glaze.

Serves 4

Red Hot Maple Glaze

6 tablespoons maple syrup

4 tablespoons hot sauce (such as Frank's RedHot)

2 tablespoons unsalted butter

1 teaspoon Dijon mustard

Combine all the ingredients in a saucepan and heat over medium heat. Cook until the glaze is warm and the butter is melted. Reduce to a syrupy consistency.

Makes 1/2 cup

GREASE WAS THE WAY

Pat After you fry something on the stovetop, what do you do with the grease? The mind-set in our household was never to let anything go to waste. Mama Rena kept a tin can with a hole-punched metal lid on top. Once she was finished frying potatoes or meats, she would pour the grease into the tin can. When she was ready to reuse the grease, she would pour it into the skillet, leaving on the lid with holes to strain all of the hard particles out. This was the first grease-filtering system I was exposed to. Pretty neat!

Blackened Catfish with Creole Rémoulade

Pat One of my favorite activities when I was a child was fishing with my grandfather Dye. You could see the excitement in his eyes the night before a fishing trip as he organized our rods, bait, and tackle boxes. We didn't have fancy fishing rods, just those old cane poles with lightweight red bulbs on them. They were so long they hung out of the back window of Dye's '68 Chevrolet. After spending the morning on the banks of the Mississippi, we would return home and present our catch to Mama Rena, who was always waiting with a hot skillet ready to cook the catfish for dinner. It didn't get any better than those fishing trips with Dye, and it definitely didn't get any better than those dinners.

In Mama Rena's house, we only had our catfish one way: fried, and served with hot sauce and her homemade slaw. My first taste of blackened catfish didn't come until college, but, boy, was it delicious—even without the breading!

For this recipe, make sure you use a cast-iron skillet, just like Mama Rena. Your peanut oil must be hot, but not so hot that you burn the outside of the fish before it cooks all the way through. We recommend medium to high heat. To create the blackened crust, make sure to season your fish fully. For this dish, we threw together paprika, thyme, onion powder, garlic, and some cayenne to produce one helluva seasoning.

We finish this catfish off with such a great dipping sauce that the fish might actually think it's returning to the Mississippi River. The Creole mustard is the star of this sauce, and we add a dash of hot sauce to kick it up a notch. This dish is super-dear to my heart, 'cause it brings back wonderful memories of the summer days that I spent with Dye and Mama Rena.

---

2 tablespoons smoked paprika
2 tablespoons ground dried thyme
2 teaspoons onion powder
2 teaspoons garlic powder
1½ teaspoons kosher salt

½ teaspoon cayenne pepper
Four 6-ounce catfish fillets
2 tablespoons peanut oil
Rémoulade Sauce (recipe follows)
Lemon wedges, for serving

Whisk together all the blackening spices (paprika, thyme, onion powder, garlic powder, salt, and cayenne) in a small casserole dish. Dredge the fish through the spices.

Heat a large cast-iron skillet over medium-high heat. Add the peanut oil, and when it's hot and shimmers, add the catfish fillets in two batches, cooking on each side for 3 minutes. It's important to flip the fish just once to allow the seasonings to cook into your catfish and create the blackened look.

Serve with rémoulade sauce and lemon wedges.

Rémoulade Sauce

½ cup mayonnaise
¼ cup Creole mustard

Juice of ½ lemon
Dash of hot sauce

Mix all ingredients together. Cover, and refrigerate until ready to use.

Makes ¾ cup

Halibut with Kale and Mushrooms

Gina I love seafood and recently looked beyond the Southern staples like catfish, whiting, and buffalo fish in search of something new. What I discovered was halibut, and it has quickly become one of our favorite fish to cook. It's great fried, because it's a heartier fish.

3 tablespoons olive oil, plus more
    if needed
8 ounces button mushrooms, quartered
Kosher salt and freshly ground
    black pepper
1 shallot, finely chopped

3 cloves garlic, chopped
1 small bunch kale, center stems
    removed, chopped
½ cup white wine
Two 6-ounce halibut fillets, boneless
    and skinless

Heat a large skillet over medium-high heat. Pour in the oil, and once it shimmers, add the mushrooms and sauté until lightly browned, 3 to 4 minutes (sometimes you need an extra drizzle of oil while sautéing mushrooms, but always start out with just 3 tablespoons). Season with salt and pepper. Drop in the shallot, garlic, and kale by handfuls and cook, stirring, for 5 to 6 minutes, or until the kale is soft. Season the halibut fillets on both sides with salt and pepper. Pour in the wine, and nestle the halibut fillets into the kale. Turn down the heat to medium, cover the skillet with a tight-fitting lid, and steam the fillets for 8 to 9 minutes, or until the fish flakes easily and looks opaque. Serve the halibut on a bed of kale and mushrooms.

Serves 2

Smoked Sausage Shrimp and Grits

Gina All Southern cooks have tried their hands at shrimp and grits, and each one has his or her own version of the dish. My mom used to season her shrimp with garlic and onion and just prepare the grits with a little salt and pepper. Pat remembers his aunt Leona adding a little pig to her version. Once I heard that, I had to try it, too. Grits don't have much flavor on their own, but they absorb the flavor of whatever they're cooked with. With the cream cheese, Parmesan, shrimp, and sausage, there's plenty of flavor to go around in this dish.

GRITS

4 cups homemade or low-sodium
 store-bought chicken broth

1 cup quick-cooking grits

3 ounces cream cheese, cubed

2 tablespoons grated Parmesan cheese

3 tablespoons unsalted butter

Kosher salt and freshly ground
 black pepper

SHRIMP AND SAUSAGE

1 tablespoon unsalted butter

1 tablespoon olive oil

6 ounces andouille sausage, sliced,
 then roughly chopped

½ Vidalia onion, chopped

1 red bell pepper, seeded and chopped

3 cloves garlic, chopped

1¼ pounds large shrimp, peeled and
 deveined

One 14.5-ounce can diced tomatoes,
 juices drained

½ cup white wine

2 tablespoons heavy cream

Green onions, sliced, for serving

Hot sauce, optional

Bring the chicken broth to a simmer in a medium saucepan. Pour in the grits, whisking constantly. Keep stirring as the grits return to a low simmer and become thick, about 5 minutes. Stir in the cream cheese, Parmesan, and the 3 tablespoons butter. Season the grits with salt and pepper to taste. Cover with a lid, and turn the heat down to low to keep the grits warm.

Melt the 1 tablespoon butter and heat the olive oil in a large heavy-bottomed sauté pan over medium-high heat. Once it's foamy, add the sausage, and cook until browned around the edges, 3 to 4 minutes. Toss in the onion and bell pepper, and cook until soft, about 5 minutes more. Add the garlic, and sauté until fragrant, just 1 minute. Stir in the shrimp, and cook, stirring, for 2 minutes. Remove shrimp to a plate. Pour in the diced tomatoes, white wine, and heavy cream, and simmer over medium heat for 5 to 7 minutes, until thickened. Stir shrimp back into the sauce, taste for seasoning, and adjust as necessary.

Serve the shrimp over a nice mound of creamy grits, and top with green onions. Pass around hot sauce, if you like.

Serves 4

Smoked and Grilled

Grilled Salmon with Peach Relish

Apple, Bacon, and Bourbon Stuffed Pork Chops

Smoked and Spicy Chicken Wings

Grilled Sausage and Pepper Sandwich

Smoked Catfish with Lemon and Dill

Brown Sugar and Soy–Marinated Flank Steak

Grilled Turkey Breast with Mayonnaise Marinade and Mop Sauce

BBQ'd Slaw Dog

Easy Grilled Veggie Platter with Champagne Vinaigrette

Smoky Grilled Corn in the Husk

Pat When I was growing up, there was never anything better than hanging out in the backyard with Daddy Milton while he set up his grill. Once he got the fire started, he would sit in a chair and wait until the temperature was just right. While he waited, he'd share stories about his childhood in the country, and how his father used to smoke whole hogs over a big fire. Barbecue must be in my blood, because I love to grill. Throughout these next recipes, you'll learn when to use your gas grill and when it's necessary to use your smoker.

We've included a great grilled-corn recipe that takes me right back to driving down the rural roads of Memphis, staring at endless cornfields on either side. Corn is strong enough to withstand the intense heat of the grill and is such a simple addition to your summertime BBQ. I often throw it on the top shelf of my grill while my meats are cooking on the bottom rack. The smoky aroma from the grill adds just the right flavor. We've also included recipes from stuffed pork chops to grilled salmon and smoked catfish, so go get grilling!

Grilled Salmon with Peach Relish

Pat The first step to grilling any fish is to clean your grill. Then preheat the grill, and once it's hot, wipe down the grates with a tea towel that has been dipped in oil. Fish is more delicate than other meats, and this will prevent it from sticking to the grates. Salmon is a thicker cut of fish that can withstand intense heat, so it's one of the best fish to grill. To balance the smoky flavor, Gina and I created a sweet peach relish to top our salmon. We use fresh peaches, red onion, and jalapeño for the right amount of spice. The best part of this dish is how easy it is to prepare. The relish can even be made the night before, and the fish needs only a few minutes on the grill. It goes well with Gina's Quick Confetti Collards (page 64).

---

2 firm but ripe peaches, chopped into small pieces
½ small red onion, finely chopped
1 jalapeño, seeded and finely diced
Juice of ½ lime

1 teaspoon sugar
Kosher salt and freshly ground black pepper
Four 6-ounce salmon fillets
Olive oil, for grill

Combine the peaches, onion, jalapeño, lime juice, and sugar in a small bowl. Season with salt and pepper, and let stand at room temperature while you prepare the salmon.

Heat grill to medium-high heat.

Season the salmon fillets on both sides with salt and pepper. Using a clean tea towel, wipe grill grates with olive oil. Grill salmon on each side for 4 minutes. Serve topped with peach relish.

Serves 4

Apple, Bacon, and Bourbon Stuffed Pork Chops

Pat For years, I thought the only way to cook pork chops was to fry the hell out of them. That was the way my mother and grandmothers prepared them. Even when they made pork-chop soup (which is a recipe in our first cookbook, *Down Home with the Neelys*), they fried the pork chops first. As I started to improve my grilling skills, I realized the grill brought out flavors in pork chops that frying them didn't. Pork is naturally salty, and goes really well with the sweetness of the Granny Smith apples in our stuffing. For the stuffing, keep in mind that you will have to do a little outpatient surgery, so be sure to tell your butcher the chops must be at least 1½ inches thick. If you are afraid of having the stuffing fall out, pin the chops closed, using toothpicks. Gina and I call this recipe "Grown Folks' Chops," because of the bourbon we add to our stuffing. We'll invite a few couples over during the fall season and have a nice cozy dinner in the backyard with a salad, grilled corn, and one of Gina's fabulous cocktails.

5 strips bacon, sliced
½ onion, chopped
1 Granny Smith apple, diced
1 tablespoon chopped fresh sage
Kosher salt and freshly ground
   black pepper

2 tablespoons bourbon
Four 1½-inch-thick bone-in pork-loin
   chops (12 ounces each)

In a large skillet, cook the bacon over medium heat. After 3 minutes, remove some of the rendered fat and add the onion. Sauté until soft, 3 to 4 minutes. Add the apple and sage, and cook, stirring, until the mixture turns golden brown and is very soft, about 5 minutes. Season the mixture with salt and pepper. Carefully add the bourbon, and stir up any brown bits on the bottom of the pan. Cook and stir until the pan is dry, about 2 more minutes. Remove the mixture from the pan, and cool completely.

Using a chef's knife, carefully make a slit in the side of each pork chop, creating a pocket to stuff ingredients into.

Heat grill to medium-high heat.

Season the pork chops on both sides with salt and pepper. Fill them with the stuffing, and grill for 15 to 17 minutes, flipping every few minutes to keep them from getting too dark. Remove them from the heat, and allow them to rest for 5 minutes before serving.

Serves 4

SMOKING

Pat Smoking meats and vegetables has always been one of my favorite ways to cook them. I think it should be as common as grilling, but many don't understand the basics and are intimidated by the process. Here are my tips to get you started on your own:

The art of smoking meat and vegetables involves two main components: charcoal and hardwood. Four rules to know before you begin:

1 Always use a quality charcoal.

2 Never buy a charcoal with added lighter fluid in the coals, because it can have a terrible effect on the flavor of your meat.

3 Take your time, and let your coals heat up slowly.

4 You don't need a monster fire.

There are so many wonderful flavors of wood you can select, and you'll continue to experiment with choices as you go, but here are some general guidelines:

- Hickory wood has always been my choice for smoking pork and veggies. It is strong in flavor and plentiful in the South.

- Mesquite is generally found west of Texas. It's slightly milder than hickory and is really great for beef, sausages, and chicken.

- I'm also a fan of apple, pecan, and other fruitwoods. These hardwoods will add a touch of sweetness to your vegetables and meats.

PREP THE FIRE

Usually I start by making sure all the old charcoal ashes from my last smoking session are dumped out of my smoker. I never dump them right after I'm done, because they're too hot, and if you put hot coals in the trash . . . well, get ready to call the fire department.

Once all the ashes are dumped and the bottom is clean, I add two to three medium-sized handfuls of charcoal to one side of my grill and light them. The coals are relegated to one side because when I smoke I always use an indirect-heat cooking method. Indirect cooking is simple: build your charcoals and hardwood on one side of the smoker, and place your meat on the opposite side. You never want your meat directly over the flame: it could cause your meat to cook too fast. When I'm smoking, it's always *low* and *slow*, baby!

Next, using a small bucket of water, I soak my wood chips for about 15 minutes. I do this for two reasons: I want my chips to smoke or smolder, not actually burn, and if a flame does occur, the wet wood chips will generally extinguish it.

After my grill is hot, I take a wire brush and clean the grates thoroughly. This is the best time to clean your grates, because the excess debris will pull off smoothly.

START SMOKING

Once the edges of my coals start to turn white, it's time to to add the hardwood and start cooking. I always put my meat in before the hardwood, because as it warms up the pores will open, and that's generally when you are going to get the biggest impact of smoky flavor penetrating your food. I then grab one handful of wood chips from the bucket, shake off the excess water, and evenly apply the chips across my hot coals. I add more hardwood several times throughout my cooking process. If you don't think your smoker is hot enough, just add more charcoal.

Smoked and Spicy Chicken Wing

Pat Chicken wings are extremely popular in our house, so a few years ago I started sr
my own wings and serving them with a spicy Buffalo sauce. They taste equally good v
without the sauce. (I always have to serve it both ways, because one of my girls is bou
say she doesn't want sauce on hers.) The secret to our recipe is the seasoning. We ad
little brown sugar to offset the strong flavor of the paprika, chili powder, and cayenne.
so excited about pulling out my smoker that I slip into BBQ mode early, which means I spend
the night before prepping and marinating the meat. My smoker has to be set up just right,
and I cook these babies using indirect heat (see the sidebar, page 121). You can control the
temperature of your smoker by the amount of charcoal you use. Always start off with two or
three handfuls of charcoal, and add more as needed to increase the temperature. Rotate and
flip the wings every few minutes, to ensure they're cooking evenly. Adding butter to the hot
sauce will help cut the heat, and the brown sugar will thicken it all up. If some of your guests
don't want the sauce, reserve some extra dry seasoning, and once the wings come off the
smoker, sprinkle some on while they're still hot.

---

2 teaspoons kosher salt

1 teaspoon granulated white sugar

1 teaspoon garlic powder

1 teaspoon smoked paprika

1 teaspoon chili powder

⅛ teaspoon cayenne pepper

3 pounds chicken wings, cut
   at joint

Hickory wood chips, soaked
   in water for 1 hour

SAUCE

4 tablespoons unsalted butter

¼ cup hot sauce

2 tablespoons light-brown sugar

1 tablespoon apple-cider vinegar

Mix together the dry-rub ingredients, and sprinkle them on the chicken. Cover with plastic
wrap, and refrigerate for 2 hours or up to overnight.

Heat the grill to medium-low, about 250 degrees F, using indirect heat. Place the chicken
wings on the side of the grill away from the hot coals. Sprinkle a handful of drained wood
chips over the white-hot coals. Cover with the lid, leaving a slight vent, and smoke until the
skin is golden and crisp and the meat is pulling away from the bones, about 1 hour and 45
minutes.

Melt the butter in a saucepan over medium heat, and stir in the hot sauce, brown sugar,
and apple-cider vinegar. Bring to a simmer. Transfer the sauce to a large bowl. Dredge the
cooked wings through the sauce, and serve.

Serves 4 to 6

...ed Sausage and Pepper Sandwich

... I used to grill sausages as an appetizer for Spenser and Shelbi while we waited by the grill for dinner to cook. I'd set out some grilled sausage, cubed cheddar cheese, pickle spears, and crackers as a little treat before dinner, and I'd have to be careful not to fill up too much. This ritual inspired the recipe for this sandwich. Why not make the sausage and beer the main event? Here we use bratwurst sausage and poach it in beer before putting it on the grill. Bratwurst has a tough casing, so be sure to prick a few holes in it so the sausage can absorb some of the flavor in the beer. This will also allow the smoke from the grill to penetrate and create additional flavor.

This is a great-looking sandwich, because of the variety of colors in the peppers. We use yellow, red, and orange bell peppers; grilling them keeps them juicy while still creating charred grill marks. A strong hoagie roll with our garlic butter holds everything together, and I have to warn you, you might want to cut this baby in half before you take your first bite, because it's truly a monster of a sandwich.

---

8 links bratwurst sausage (about 24 ounces total)

Two 12-ounce cans beer

1 yellow bell pepper, sliced into 1¼-inch pieces

1 red bell pepper, sliced into 1¼-inch pieces

1 orange bell pepper, sliced into 1¼-inch pieces

1 red onion, sliced into ¼-inch-thick rings

3 tablespoons unsalted butter

2 cloves garlic, chopped

4 soft hoagie or grinder rolls (each 7 inches long), split

Prick the sausage casings a few times with a paring knife. Place sausage in a saucepan, and pour in enough beer to cover the sausages. Over medium heat, bring to a gentle simmer. Poach the sausages until they are cooked through, about 6 minutes. Let them cool in the beer, and then remove from the pot with tongs and drain.

Heat grill to medium-high heat.

Split the sausages down the center. Grill until the outside is crisp, about 4 minutes on each side. Grill the bell peppers and onion until nicely golden, charred in spots, and softened, about 4 minutes on each side. Melt the butter in a small skillet. Once it's foaming, add garlic, and cook until fragrant, about 1 minute. Brush the rolls with the melted garlic butter, and toast on the grill until lightly crisp. Pile the sausage and peppers into the rolls, and serve.

Serves 4

Tip Poach the sausages up to a day ahead, and refrigerate until ready to grill.

DYE (Rufus Wright)

Pat My paternal grandfather, Dye, was refined, well dressed, and soft-spoken. He worked for the railroad as a Pullman porter, which meant he was able to travel the United States. After he retired, he worked part-time as a security officer and spent his spare time following his true passion: fishing. Catfish was always the main catch. I loved to sit on the banks of the Mississippi River with him, gently casting our fishing lines into the water. Now, fishing is a sport of patience and quiet. If you talk too loudly, you will scare away the fish. It was a perfect setting for Dye, the original man of few words. After a few casts, he always opened up and used to tell me stories about his long work trips and the different cities he'd traveled to.

Dye was happiest when he was fishing. He also helped me discover my own great passion by introducing me to barbecue. The first barbecue pit I ever saw was in Dye's backyard. The bricks were stacked about 3 feet high, and inside was a metal grate. He used to put his coals and wood underneath the grate on the bare ground. He was very proud of his homemade BBQ pit, and he loved to grill steaks, chops, and ribs. And now, because of him, so do I.

Smoked Catfish with Lemon and Dill

Pat Gina likes to have something for everyone when we're entertaining, which means I'm often out back manning a grill with pork, a few steaks, and some chicken. Several years ago, I decided to add catfish to the mix. During my first attempt, I overcooked it and the fish stuck to the grate so badly that by the time I pulled the fillets off the grill they looked more like catfish nuggets. I also used hickory chips, and the poor catfish didn't stand a chance against the strong flavor. I had to go back to the drawing board. I usually reserve my smoker for larger cuts of meat, like pork butt, spare ribs, or brisket, but I had to adjust my way of thinking for catfish. I decided to try a milder, sweeter hardwood, and applewood was the first that came to mind. I oiled the grates of the smoker, which helped keep the fillets from sticking, and kept the temperature low so they wouldn't cook too quickly. Everything must pass the "Gina taste test" before I can serve it to house guests, and when I finally got this right, Gina fell in love with the dish, and with me all over again. Jackpot, baby.

Four 8-ounce catfish fillets
1 tablespoon chopped fresh dill
Grated zest of 1 lemon
Kosher salt and freshly ground
    black pepper

Applewood chips, soaked in water
    for 1 hour, then drained
Olive oil, for grill

Season the catfish on both sides with dill, lemon zest, and salt and pepper.

Set up your grill for indirect heat at a medium-low temperature, about 250 degrees F. Sprinkle hot coals with soaked and drained applewood chips. Brush grill grates with olive oil, and set the catfish on the side of the grill away from the coals. Cover with the lid, leaving it partially vented, and smoke the catfish until it's cooked through, easily flaked, and lightly golden brown, about 1 hour.

Serves 4 to 6

Tip Smoked catfish is great served topped with a lemony mayonnaise, or in salads and sandwiches. Leftovers can be folded into dips with mayonnaise and cream cheese for a delicious appetizer.

Brown Sugar and Soy–Marinated Flank Steak

Pat We never had steak when I was growing up. It was too expensive, and my mom had too many mouths to feed. However, as a Sunday morning special, Mama Daisy sometimes used to pan-fry flank steak for Daddy Milton, my grandfather. It used to be the highlight of his week. Gina and I make steak for our family more often than Mama Daisy did, but we still try to make it something special. For the marinade in this dish, Gina uses canola oil, soy, and brown sugar. We like to marinate our steak for several hours, to build the flavor and create tenderness. Once it hits the grill, give it time to cook on each side, and only flip it once. Be sure to allow the meat to rest after pulling it off the grill, and always slice against the grain.

½ cup low-sodium soy sauce
¼ cup canola oil
3 tablespoons light-brown sugar
1 tablespoon tomato paste
1 tablespoon Worcestershire sauce

1 teaspoon red-pepper flakes
4 cloves garlic, roughly chopped
2½ pounds flank steak, trimmed
   of visible fat

Whisk together the marinade ingredients, and pour into a large ziptop bag. Add the flank steak, seal the bag, and chill in the refrigerator for at least 2 hours, or up to 8 hours. Flip the bag over halfway through marinating.

Heat grill to medium-high heat. Take the steak out of the fridge so it can warm to room temperature.

Remove the steak from the marinade, and grill for 5 minutes on each side for medium. Remove from the heat, and let rest at least 5 minutes before slicing across the grain into ½-inch-thick slices.

Serves 4 to 6

Grilled Turkey Breast with Mayonnaise Marinade and Mop Sauce

Pat It took me a few tries to perfect my smoking technique for turkey breasts. I find that an oil-based marinade works best to keep the meat moist while it's cooking. For this recipe, we use a marinade of mayonnaise and apple-cider vinegar. The ingredients work well together to keep the turkey moist and create a nice brown crust. At home and in the restaurants, we prepare the bird the night before and let it marinate overnight. Then, while we're preheating our grill, we pull the turkey from the refrigerator and let it warm to room temperature before cooking. This way it takes less time for the turkey to heat up on the grill. We cook with the lid closed for additional moisture, and mop (also called basting) every 20 minutes of the cooking process. I strongly recommend using a thermometer to check the temperature (inexpensive at the grocery store). Once the turkey flesh reaches 165 degrees F, it's done.

---

1 cup mayonnaise

¼ cup apple-cider vinegar

1 tablespoon garlic powder

1 tablespoon onion powder

¼ teaspoon cayenne pepper

Kosher salt and freshly ground
    black pepper

One 4-to-4½-pound whole turkey breast

Mix together the mayonnaise, cider vinegar, garlic powder, onion powder, cayenne, and salt and pepper. Place the turkey breast on a sheet tray, and brush generously with the marinade. Chill in the refrigerator for at least 4 hours, or up to overnight. Reserve any leftover marinade, cover with plastic wrap, and pop it into the fridge.

Set up your grill for indirect medium heat, about 350 degrees F. If using a gas grill, light grill to medium heat on one side only. Take the turkey out of the fridge so it can warm to room temperature. Season the breast with salt and pepper.

Place the turkey breast on the hot side of the grill, skin side down, for 4 to 5 minutes, or until the skin is golden brown. Once it's browned, move the turkey breast to the cooler side of the grill. Close the lid and cook for 1 hour and 45 minutes to 2 hours, mopping every 20 minutes with the reserved sauce, until the turkey reaches an internal temperature of 165 degrees F. Remove turkey from grill, and let rest for 20 minutes.

Carve into ¼-inch-thick slices, and serve.

Serves 4 to 6

DADDY MILTON (Milton Carter)

Pat Daddy Milton was my mother's father. Like most people from Memphis, he grew up in the country. Since he was the oldest of his siblings, he had to drop out of school at an early age to help take care of his mom, younger brothers, and sisters. He worked on the family farm harvesting crops and feeding the animals, and the farm provided much of what he needed to feed the family. He raised chickens, pigs, and cows and grew corn, beans, collard greens, cabbage, and potatoes.

He soon met Daisy, and they moved to Memphis to start their own family. He remained a country boy at heart, though, and often returned to his family's farm, especially as he got older. I remember one trip my brothers and I took with him in the spring. We spent the morning picking fresh vegetables to bring back home with us, and in the afternoon we watched Daddy Milton kill a hog. I remember wondering, "What the hell are we going to do with that poor pig Granddad has just killed?" But he showed us how to butcher the pig, and I was amazed to see the animal turn into the familiar cuts of meat—pork chops, ribs, and shoulder—I had seen stored in our freezer. He then taught me something I haven't forgotten: fresh pig means a great spring pig roast.

Daddy Milton had created his own grill by mounting an old hot-water tank onto legs, cutting an opening on the side, and fitting it with grates. He used to sit for hours watching his pork cook, making sure the meat wasn't directly over the flame so that it wouldn't burn. His method was my introduction to the art of cooking with indirect heat. I loved when he roasted pigs, because it meant I could stay up all night with him. Mama Daisy would yell out the door that it was time for bed, and he would reply, "Leave him alone, he is helping me." Around 1 or 2 a.m. he would go inside and come back with a pot of his yummy BBQ sauce and mop. He'd dip that mop into the sauce and brush it over this golden-brown, smoky pork shoulder. Then he would look at me and say, "Boy, this is going to be some good eating."

BBQ'd Slaw Dog

Pat I've often been accused of adding something a little extra to my dishes, and most of the time this gets me into trouble with the girls. Gina is always saying, "It's good enough, just leave it alone." They don't complain when I make these hot dogs, though, and there's just about a little of everything on these. We always have bacon and some pulled-pork leftovers in our fridge (don't you?), so these are easy to whip up on a Saturday afternoon. Throw those puppies on the grill (or a smoker), and then top them off with some tender, moist pulled pork and a drizzle of BBQ sauce. I like to serve these to my girls when we watch a movie together. Of course, this means we're all usually asleep halfway through the movie.

4 bun-length hot dogs	1 cup Low and Slow Pulled Pork
2 strips bacon, cut in half	(page 97)
Vegetable oil, for grill	1 cup Vinegar Slaw (page 82)
4 soft hot-dog buns	Drizzle of BBQ Sauce (page 99)

Heat grill to medium heat.

Wrap each hot dog with a half-slice of bacon. Secure, using toothpicks. Brush the grill grates very lightly with oil, using a clean tea towel. Grill hot dogs for 12 to 16 minutes, rotating every few minutes, until the bacon is crisp and the dogs are warmed through. Remove toothpicks, and place each dog in a bun. Top each with ¼ cup each pulled pork and slaw. Drizzle with BBQ sauce.

Serves 4

Tip Don't use thick-sliced bacon. By the time it cooks through, your dog will be burned to a crisp!

Easy Grilled Veggie Platter with Champagne Vinaigrette

Gina Shelbi was only 4 months old when I returned to work, and we struggled finding someone to take care of her. When Nana found out about our dilemma, she called immediately and said she would take care of her for as long as we needed. She cared for Shelbi right up until preschool. She had an incredible backyard garden and Shelbi spent a lot of time helping her water and harvest her vegetables. Of course, she needed a bath most nights when we got home, but that was all right, because she grew to love veggies and we never had to force her to eat them. Nana used to give us bags of fresh veggies when we'd pick Shelbi up, and we'd often throw them on the grill. All you need is olive oil, salt, and pepper.

2 portobello mushrooms, stems removed, sliced into 1½-inch strips

2 medium zucchini, sliced lengthwise into 4½-inch-long strips

1 small eggplant, sliced into ½-inch rounds

1 medium red onion, cut into ½-inch rings

1 yellow bell pepper, seeded and cut into 1½-inch-thick strips

1 red bell pepper, seeded and cut into 1½-inch-thick strips

1 bunch asparagus, ends trimmed

3 tablespoons olive oil

Kosher salt and freshly ground black pepper

DRESSING

1 garlic clove, finely chopped

2 teaspoons Dijon mustard

2 tablespoons champagne vinegar

¼ cup olive oil

Kosher salt and freshly ground black pepper

2 tablespoons chopped fresh parsley

Heat grill to medium-high heat.

Arrange the veggies on a sheet tray. Brush both sides with the olive oil, and season with salt and pepper.

Grill the vegetables in batches until they are tender and lightly charred—5 minutes on each side for the mushrooms, 4 minutes on each side for the zucchini, eggplant, onion, and bell peppers, and 2 to 3 minutes on each side for the asparagus. Remove to a platter when finished.

Combine the garlic, mustard, and vinegar in a small bowl. Pour in the olive oil while whisking. Season with salt and pepper, and whisk in the parsley.

Drizzle the dressing over the arranged vegetables.

Serves 6

Tip These can be made hours in advance and served at room temperature—and they still taste great.

Smoky Grilled Corn in the Husk

Pat Somehow, some way, corn makes its way into a dish almost every time I turn on my grill. I usually cook my shucked corn on the top shelf of my grill while the meats cook on the bottom, so it picks up some of the flavor from the charcoal. Gina and I have prepared corn countless ways, but one of our favorites is to peel back the husk, season the kernels with butter and spices, then fold the husk back over the buttered kernels, to keep in the moisture and flavor. A lot of people soak their corn in water before grilling, but we find skipping that step gives the corn a smokier flavor.

---

4 ears corn
4 tablespoons unsalted butter, softened
1 tablespoon light-brown sugar
1 teaspoon smoked paprika

¼ teaspoon cayenne pepper
Kosher salt and freshly ground
  black pepper

Heat grill to medium-high heat.

Peel down the corn husks without removing them from the bottom of the cobs. Pluck and brush away all the fine silks from the cobs.

Combine the softened butter, brown sugar, paprika, cayenne, and salt and pepper in a small bowl. Smear the butter all over the corn, and fold back the husk, to cover the corn.

Grill the corn for 25 minutes, turning every few minutes or so. To serve, peel away the charred husks.

Serves 4

NANA (Alta Lemon)

Gina Nana lived across the street from my great-grandmother Mama Callie, and we considered her a part of our family. We spent a significant amount of time at her house—especially in her backyard garden. She grew the most beautiful roses, and just about every vegetable you can think of. Nana taught me the importance of presentation and continually influenced the way I entertained, especially when Pat and I started to work together and I ran the catering division of Neely's BBQ. Pat and I are grateful to have had Nana in our lives for countless reasons.

Sandwiches

Pat's Turkey Patty Melt

Sloppy Roast Beef Po' Boy with Debris Gravy

Fried Chicken Sandwich

Grilled Vidalia Onion and Portobello Burgers with Smoked Mozzarella
and Roasted Red Pepper Spread

WTF Burger

Pat Y'all knew we would throw in a chapter with some outstanding sandwiches like a turkey spin on a classic patty melt, and a WTF Burger that is so full-flavor we had to add it to the menu of our New York restaurant, Neely's Barbecue Parlor. Sandwiches are one of those universal dishes that can be served any time of day, and to any specification. There are an endless number of spreads and condiments, and add-ins from jalapeños to blue cheese contribute a lot of flavor and texture. And don't get me started on the bread options. We encourage you to use our recipes as blueprints and get creative with the way you prepare your sandwiches.

Pat's Turkey Patty Melt

Pat A patty melt is a classic grilled Southern sandwich with a meat patty, cheese, and sautéed veggies. My mom used to make them for us as a "halftime" treat when my brothers and I played sandlot football in the backyard. She'd call us into the house and have hot patty melts and bowls of soup waiting for us. Once we polished it all off, we'd head back out for the second half of the game.

For our recipe, we substituted ground turkey for the traditional beef patty. We piled on sautéed vegetables, and the sweetness from the red onion and the bite from the garlic really give the melt its flavor. After you've built your sandwich, butter the outside of the bread and throw it on the skillet to toast both sides and melt the cheese. Game on!

---

3 tablespoons olive oil, divided

1 small red onion, sliced

3 cloves garlic, finely chopped

Kosher salt and freshly ground
  black pepper

10 ounces ground turkey

4 tablespoons unsalted butter, softened

4 slices rye bread

¼ cup Thousand Island Dressing,
  plus more for dipping (recipe follows)

4 deli slices Swiss cheese

In a medium nonstick skillet, heat 1 tablespoon olive oil over medium-high heat. Add the onion, and sauté until browned, about 10 minutes, turning heat down if it starts to cook too fast. Add the chopped garlic for the last minute of sautéing. Season with salt and pepper, and remove to a bowl. Cover loosely with tinfoil to keep warm.

Form the meat into two 5-ounce ¼-inch-thick oval-shaped patties, roughly the same size as your bread. Generously season the patties with salt and pepper.

Wipe out the inside of the skillet you cooked the onion in, and reheat the pan with remaining 2 tablespoons olive oil over medium-high heat. Cook the patties for 3 minutes on each side, or until cooked through and no longer pink in the center.

To assemble the patty melts, butter four slices of bread. Generously spread the unbuttered side of two slices with 1 tablespoon of Thousand Island dressing. Then, on each of the dressed slices, pile on 2 slices of Swiss, a patty, and a mound of onion, and sandwich it all together with the other two slices of bread, buttered side out.

Heat a 12-inch nonstick or cast-iron skillet over medium-high heat. Griddle the sandwiches on both sides, until the bread is golden brown and all the cheese is melted, about 3 minutes per side.

Serve with extra Thousand Island Dressing for dipping.

Makes 2 sandwiches

Thousand Island Dressing

½ cup mayonnaise

3 tablespoons ketchup

1 tablespoon Sweet Pickled Relish
(page 10)

Kosher salt and freshly ground
black pepper

Dash of Worcestershire sauce

Combine all ingredients in a bowl.

Makes ¾ cup

Sloppy Roast Beef Po' Boy with Debris Gravy

Pat There's nothing like a great big slow-cooked "roast," as my mom always called roast beef. I grew up eating plenty of it, so I should know. Gina used to laugh at me when I prepared my mom's roast for us shortly after we got married. She thought I was nuts (she still might). Gina's version of roast involved slowly cooking it in a Dutch oven and adding chunks of potatoes and carrots toward the end of the cooking process. My version was similar, only I add a little more stuff. Okay, a lot more stuff. I add corn, peas, tomatoes, chopped okra, onion, and anything else I can find. I love making sandwiches with the leftovers, and eventually I got tired of waiting for leftovers to make a great roast-beef sandwich so Gina and I decided to braise a roast beef strictly for a good ole New Orleans–style sandwich.

---

2 tablespoons vegetable oil
2¾ pounds beef chuck roast
Kosher salt and freshly ground
    black pepper
1½ teaspoons Cajun seasoning, divided
1 onion, roughly chopped
6 cloves garlic, smashed, peeled,
    and roughly chopped
3 sprigs fresh thyme

1 cup red wine
3 cups homemade or low-sodium
    store-bought chicken stock
Dash of Worcestershire sauce
One 24-inch soft French baguette
    (an 8-ounce loaf)
Mayonnaise, shredded iceberg lettuce,
    sliced tomatoes, sliced dill pickles,
    and hot sauce, for topping

Heat the oil in a large high-sided skillet or braiser over medium-high heat. Season the chuck roast generously on both sides with salt, pepper, and 1 teaspoon of Cajun seasoning (it's always better to season overnight, if you have time). Sear the roast on both sides until well browned, about 10 minutes total. Remove to a plate.

Toss in the onion, garlic, and thyme, and sauté for 4 minutes, until soft and beginning to brown. Sprinkle in the remaining ½ teaspoon Cajun seasoning for the last minute of cooking. Stir in the wine, and scrape up any browned bits on the bottom of the pan. Bring to a boil, and cook until the harsh wine smell is gone, about 2 minutes. Stir in the stock, bring to a simmer, and season with salt and pepper. Add the roast back to the pan with any accumulated juices that may be on the plate. Turn heat to low, and cover with a tight-fitting lid. Cook, flipping the meat on occasion, for 3 hours and 30 minutes, or until the meat begins to fall apart.

Check on the meat, and once it's tender, use tongs to break it up into chunks. It should practically fall apart on its own. Stir in the Worcestershire sauce, and bring the sauce to a simmer. Reduce the sauce until it's thick and coats the back of a spoon like gravy, about 20 minutes. Remove the thyme sprigs, and skim off all of the visible fat floating on the surface. Taste for seasoning, and adjust accordingly.

Split the baguette in half lengthwise, and cut the bread into six 4-inch pieces. Brush both sides of the bread generously with mayonnaise; pile the bottoms with meat and gravy, lettuce, tomatoes, pickles, and a few dashes of hot sauce. Smush the top of the bread over the meat, and enjoy the sloppiness.

Makes six 4-inch po' boys

Fried Chicken Sandwich

Pat   A lot of people raised chickens in my grandparents' old neighborhood. They had chicken coops set up in the backyard, and there was always a fresh supply of eggs. Our family friend Ne-ne, who lived across the street from my grandparents, had several. We used to love going over to her house to chase the chickens around her yard while she'd yell for us to quit bothering them. Every morning, she went out, her apron pockets filled with corn and wheat, to feed them and collect eggs. Every once in a while she'd process a chicken and cook some of the best chicken dinners I've ever tasted. This sandwich reminds me of her, and I wish I could spend an afternoon on her porch, watching those crazy chickens run around.

One 8-ounce skinless, boneless chicken
    breast, sliced in half horizontally
Kosher salt and freshly ground
    black pepper
2 large eggs
1 tablespoon hot sauce
1 tablespoon water
½ cup all-purpose flour
1 teaspoon paprika
½ teaspoon garlic powder
¼ teaspoon cayenne pepper
Peanut oil, for frying
2 tablespoons unsalted butter, softened
2 soft sandwich rolls, split
Mayonnaise, sliced tomatoes, shredded
    iceberg lettuce, sliced bread-and-
    butter pickles, and sliced pickled
    banana peppers, for topping

Pound the chicken with a rubber mallet to an even thickness, about ½ inch thick. Season the cutlets on both sides with salt and pepper. Whisk together the eggs, hot sauce, and water in a pie plate. In a second pie plate, whisk together the flour, paprika, garlic powder, and cayenne.

Heat 2 inches of the oil in a large high-sided cast-iron skillet over medium-high heat until a deep-fry thermometer reaches 350 degrees F.

Dip the chicken into the egg on both sides, letting excess drip off, then into flour mixture, dusting off excess. Dip the chicken back into the egg, then into the flour, making a double breading. Add both chicken pieces to the hot oil, and cook until golden and browned, 4 to 5 minutes, flipping about halfway through cooking. Remove to a paper-towel-lined plate to drain and cool slightly.

Heat a nonstick or cast-iron skillet over medium-high heat. Butter the inside of both the rolls, and toast in the hot skillet until golden and browned.

Generously brush both pieces of each toasted roll with mayo. Top the roll bottoms with chicken breasts, tomato, lettuce, pickles, and pickled banana peppers, and sandwich all together.

Makes 2

Grilled Vidalia Onion and Portobello Burgers with Smoked Mozzarella and Roasted Red Pepper Spread

Gina You may be surprised to see a portobello burger from the first family of barbecue, but this burger is so good you won't miss the meat—I promise.

---

2 large portobello-mushroom caps, stems removed

Two ½-inch-thick slices Vidalia onion

3 tablespoons olive oil

Kosher salt and freshly ground black pepper

4 thick slices smoked mozzarella cheese

2 tablespoons unsalted butter, softened

2 soft hamburger buns with sesame seeds, split

Roasted Red Pepper Spread (recipe follows)

Baby arugula, for topping

Heat grill to medium-high heat.

Drizzle the mushroom caps and onion slices with olive oil, and season with salt and pepper. Grill until golden and browned, 4 to 6 minutes on each side for the mushrooms, and 4 minutes on each side for the onion. While everything is still on the grill, place the grilled onion on top of the mushrooms, then top with mozzarella cheese, so the cheese will ooze and melt over the mushrooms. Butter the buns, and grill for 1 minute, until toasted.

Build the burger by brushing both sides of each bun with red-pepper spread, topping the bottoms with grilled mushroom, piling on the arugula, and sandwiching with the top of the bun.

Makes 2

Roasted Red Pepper Spread

¼ cup chopped roasted red bell peppers, drained well

¼ cup mayonnaise

⅛ teaspoon cayenne pepper

Kosher salt and freshly ground black pepper

Blend all the ingredients in a food processor until smooth. Taste, and adjust seasoning with salt and pepper.

Makes ½ cup

WTF Burger

Pat I know what you are thinking: WTF? What's This Flavor, right? For years, I used to season my ground beef burgers with a store-bought seasoning and throw them on the grill. I couldn't understand why they puffed up until I was told to take my thumb and press a small indent into the center of the patties before placing them on the grill. This keeps them from expanding and creates a little puddle, so the juices remain in the center of the patty, for extra flavor. I don't think my grandmother understood this, because her burgers were always so puffy that by my second bite my bread was so soaked I couldn't pick it up. It was messy, but packed with flavor and oh so good.

Mixing shallot, salt, and pepper into the ground beef before forming the patties will help season the meat from the inside as it cooks. To keep Gina happy, we added a little pig and threw on some pulled pork and bacon. Next time you are having guests over for grilled burgers, put this monster sandwich together and they will all be asking WTF.

1¾ pounds ground chuck
1 small shallot, finely chopped
Kosher salt and freshly ground
   black pepper
4 deli slices pepper-jack cheese
4 deli slices white cheddar
4 brioche buns, split and buttered

4 strips bacon, cooked crisp,
   broken in half
¾ pound Low and Slow Pulled Pork
   (page 97)
¼ cup BBQ Sauce (page 99)
Shredded lettuce, sliced tomato,
   and red onion, for topping

Heat grill to medium-high heat.

In a large mixing bowl, break up the meat with a wooden spoon. Sprinkle in the chopped shallot, and generously season with salt and pepper. Toss together, trying not to overwork it (overworked meat will be tough). Divide the meat into four equal-sized balls. Flatten them into ¾-inch-thick patties, and use your thumb to create a shallow indentation in the center of each burger.

Grill the burgers for 3 to 4 minutes. Flip, and continue to cook for another 4 minutes. Top the patties with the cheese, and toast the buns for the last minute of grilling.

Assemble the burgers by piling on the bacon, pulled pork, barbecue sauce, lettuce, tomato, and onion.

Makes 4 burgers

Casseroles, Soups, and Stews

Remixed Green Bean Casserole

Old-Fashioned Elbow Mac and Cheese

Chicken Pot Pie

Three-Cheese Pasta Bake with Spinach

Tomato Bisque

Big Pot of Chicken and Sausage Gumbo

Veggie Tortilla Soup

Corn and Crab Chowder

Brunswick Stew

Lemony Chicken and Kale Soup

Gina One-pot dinners, such as casseroles, soups, and stews, are a big part of Southern culinary tradition. Food is a comfort to Southerners, and it has long been common to bring someone a casserole or stew to show you care.

Casseroles, soups, and stews are easy to warm up, and there's no need to prepare anything else. Pat and I both grew up in single-mother households, and our mothers did what they could to make sure we had a big dinner every night. Pat's mom, Lorine, used to start her Crock-Pot in the morning, before she went to work, so, by the time she got home at night, dinner was hot and ready to be served. Pat and I recognized the brilliance in this when Spenser and Shelbi were young and we were both working full-time. A one-pot dinner meant less time spent over the stove, less time cleaning, and more time with each other.

Remixed Green Bean Casserole

Gina I grew up eating my mom's green-bean casserole. You know, the same one you grew up eating, with the onions on top? This dish has been around for ages, so I decided to revisit the classic recipe and update it to something my family would really love. My girls are big fans of mushrooms, so my first step was to add them to the base of the casserole. I asked my girls to help me trim the ends off, and it reminded me of when I used to help my mom prepare dinner. It's fun to pass my mom's cooking techniques on to Spenser and Shelbi and know that eventually they will do the same for their daughters.

Kosher salt

1¼ pounds green beans, trimmed, halved

2 tablespoons unsalted butter

1 tablespoon olive oil

12 ounces mushrooms, sliced

1 shallot, finely chopped

3 cloves garlic, finely chopped

1 teaspoon chopped fresh thyme leaves

2 tablespoons all-purpose flour

1 cup homemade or low-sodium store-bought chicken broth

¾ cup heavy cream

¼ cup grated Parmesan cheese

2 cups French's French Fried Onions

Preheat oven to 350 degrees F.

Bring a large pot of salted water to a boil. Add the green beans, and cook for 3 minutes, until bright green and crisp-tender. Drain, and rinse under cold water until they are cool.

Heat the butter and oil in a large skillet over medium heat. Once the butter is foaming, add the mushrooms, and cook, stirring, until they are browned, about 5 minutes. Stir in the shallot, garlic, and thyme, and cook for 1 minute. Sprinkle in the flour, and cook, stirring, for another minute. Pour in the broth, and stir well until no lumps remain. Bring to a boil, then reduce to a simmer, and stir in the heavy cream. Simmer for 4 minutes, until thick. Stir in the green beans, and mix well.

Add the green-bean mixture to a 2-quart casserole dish, sprinkle with the Parmesan cheese, and top with the fried onions. Bake for 20 minutes, or until bubbling with a golden-brown crust.

Serves 6

Tip The casserole can be prepared a day earlier and baked the day of eating. Just bring back to room temperature, top with Parmesan cheese and onions, and bake as directed.

GINA'S MOM (Erma Jean Ervin)

Gina My mom was a single parent for most of my life. She managed to work, raise five children, and always have food on the table for us. It wasn't always an elaborately planned meal, but she put a lot of love into everything she made for us and did the best with what she had. I was the youngest; my older siblings, especially my sister Kim, stepped in and it felt like I had a village of people taking care of me.

By example, my mom taught me the importance of family, getting good food on the table no matter what, and making the best of your circumstances. I'm forever grateful for the strength and perseverance I inherited from her.

Old-Fashioned Elbow Mac and Cheese

Pat Most people have a favorite way to prepare macaroni and cheese, and they stick to it. My mom uses sharp cheddar as her base, and then bakes off a golden-brown crust. Gina's sister Tanya, on the other hand, uses at least four or five different cheeses. Gina and I have experimented with everything from bacon and kettle chips to lobster in search of our reigning favorite, and I think we've finally found it. The base of our cheese sauce is simple—just milk, cheese, and flour—and we add a little kick with garlic powder, mustard powder, and cayenne pepper. The sauce may seem thin once you add the milk, but it will thicken with the starch from the noodles as they bake. Our secret ingredient is the Ritz-cracker breadcrumbs, which add a saltiness to the dish that regular breadcrumbs don't.

Butter, for the dish

8 ounces elbow macaroni (half a 1-pound box)

2 cups whole milk

¼ cup all-purpose flour

1 teaspoon garlic powder

1 teaspoon mustard powder

⅛ teaspoon cayenne pepper

Dash of Worcestershire sauce

Kosher salt and freshly ground black pepper

16 ounces sharp cheddar cheese, shredded (4 cups), divided

1 cup crushed Ritz crackers

Preheat oven to 350 degrees F. Lightly grease a 2-quart casserole dish.

Bring a large pot of salted water to a boil. Add the elbow macaroni, and cook as indicated in package instructions. Drain.

In a large bowl, whisk together the milk, flour, garlic powder, mustard powder, cayenne, Worcestershire sauce, and salt and pepper until smooth. Stir in 3½ cups cheese and cooked macaroni. Pour the macaroni into the prepared baking dish. Sprinkle surface with crushed Ritz crackers and remaining cheese. Bake for 35 minutes, or until golden and bubbly.

Serves 6

Tip Make sure not to overcook the noodles, and keep in mind you'll be putting this casserole back into the oven to bake off, so the noodles will continue to cook then as well.

Chicken Pot Pie

Pat I had to do a little research to find out why this dish is called "chicken pot pie." I get the chicken and the pie part, but "pot"? It was an English tradition to make a meat pie by molding the dough on the bottom of a pot, baking it, then removing the molded pastry from the pot before filling it with meat and vegetables and topping it with more pastry. The result was a pastry "pot pie." All very interesting, but this dish is something I look forward to eating regardless of what it's cooked in. I could eat it every day as a child, and my mother always served it with homemade applesauce. (Yes, you read that right. Give it a try!) One of the things that I love about casseroles and stews is that there are no rules. You can add anything you want to the recipe and really make it your own. If you prefer to use turkey instead of chicken for this, go for it. Remember, I told you there were no rules. The thyme, garlic, onion, and celery are all the seasoning you need. Let me tell you something—when you pull this baby out of the oven and sit down to enjoy the meal, you won't care where the "pot" in this chicken pot pie came from, either.

---

1 sheet frozen puff pastry
  (from a 17.3-ounce box)
2 bone-in, skin-on chicken breasts
  (about 2 pounds)
4 cups homemade or low-sodium
  store-bought chicken broth
4 tablespoons salted butter
1 medium onion, finely chopped
3 medium carrots, cut into
  ½-inch rounds

3 stalks celery, sliced
2 cloves garlic, finely chopped
1 teaspoon chopped fresh
  thyme leaves
½ cup all-purpose flour
¼ cup heavy cream
10 ounces frozen peas
Egg wash (1 egg beaten with
  1 tablespoon water)

Preheat oven to 400 degrees F. Thaw your puff pastry.

Add both chicken breasts to a large saucepan, and cover with broth. Bring broth up to a boil, reduce to a low simmer, and cover with a tight-fitting lid. Cook the chicken for 15 minutes, or until it's cooked through. Using tongs, remove the chicken to a plate until cool enough to handle. Remove skin, then shred the chicken with a fork and chop into bite-sized pieces. Reserve the chicken and broth, and discard bones.

In a large skillet, melt the butter over medium heat. Add the onion, carrots, and celery, and sauté until tender, about 6 minutes. Add the garlic and thyme, and cook 1 more minute. Sprinkle in the flour, and cook, stirring, for about 2 minutes. Ladle in the hot broth and heavy cream. Bring to a boil, then reduce to a simmer, and cook for 10 minutes, until the sauce is thick. Stir in the chicken and peas to warm.

Transfer the mixture to a 2½-quart round casserole dish. Unfold the puff pastry and place over the top. Use a fork to crimp edges, and cut a hole in the top by making an "X" and folding back the sides. Brush the pastry with egg wash. Bake for 20 minutes, until golden and browned.

Serves 6

Three-Cheese Pasta Bake with Spinach

Gina As we said before, there are many variations of mac and cheese, and everyone has a preference for what they like best. But how can you go wrong with (three!) melted cheeses, pasta, turkey, and spinach? Quick answer: you can't.

Nonstick spray

Kosher salt and freshly ground
    black pepper

12 ounces whole-wheat rotini
    (regular would be fine, too)

1 tablespoon olive oil

1 large onion, chopped

¾ pound ground lean turkey

3 cloves garlic, finely chopped

Big pinch of red-pepper flakes

One 28-ounce can crushed tomatoes

¼ cup basil leaves, torn

One 8-ounce bunch spinach,
    stems removed, chopped

2 cups shredded part-skim mozzarella
    cheese, divided

1 cup part-skim ricotta cheese

¼ cup Parmesan cheese

Preheat oven to 375 degrees F. Spray a 13-by-9-inch baking dish with nonstick spray.

Bring a large pot of salted water to a boil. Add the pasta, and cook until al dente, about 1 minute less than the package instructions. Drain pasta, and put it in a large bowl.

Heat the olive oil in a large high-sided skillet over medium-high heat. Once it's hot, add the onion, and sauté until softened, about 4 minutes. Add the turkey and garlic, and cook, stirring, until browned and crumbly, another 4 minutes. Add a big pinch of red-pepper flakes to the last minute of cooking, and season the mixture well with salt and pepper. Stir in the tomatoes, reduce heat to medium, and simmer for 10 minutes. Turn off the heat, stir in the basil leaves, taste, and adjust seasoning as necessary.

To the pasta, add the spinach, tomato sauce, 1½ cups of mozzarella, and the ricotta. Pour the mixture into the prepared baking dish, and sprinkle with the remaining ½ cup mozzarella and the Parmesan. Bake for 25 minutes, or until the top is golden and the cheese is melted.

Serves 6 to 8

Tomato Bisque

Gina When I was younger, everyone on my block grew tomatoes in their backyard gardens.
I loved them so much I used to eat them with just salt and pepper. This creamy bisque recipe
lets the fresh tomatoes really shine as the primary flavor of the soup.

2 tablespoons unsalted butter

1 red onion, chopped

2 carrots, chopped

3 cloves garlic, chopped

Kosher salt and freshly ground
  black pepper

3 cups homemade or low-sodium
  store-bought chicken broth

One 28-ounce can whole peeled
  tomatoes

1 teaspoon sugar

¼ cup packed chopped fresh basil
  leaves, plus more for garnish

½ cup heavy cream

Melt the butter in a large saucepan over medium heat. Add onion, carrots, and garlic, and
sauté until softened, about 6 minutes. Season with salt and pepper. Add the chicken broth,
tomatoes, and sugar, bring to a boil, then reduce heat and simmer for 15 to 20 minutes,
until vegetables are tender. Toss in the basil, and purée in a blender until smooth. Stir in the
heavy cream, and taste for seasoning. Add more salt and pepper as needed. Serve in warm
bowls with some fresh basil leaves on top.

Serves 4 to 6

Big Pot of Chicken and Sausage Gumbo

Pat My aunt Barbara made me my first bowl of gumbo, and I've been a fan ever since. Gumbo is a heartier soup—a mix between a soup and a stew—and it's packed with New Orleans flavor and spice. Aunt Barbara developed her recipe when she lived in New Orleans and brought it back to Memphis with her. She made a seafood gumbo with crab, shrimp, and crawfish and had a mean red-beans-and-rice recipe to go with it. I get hungry just thinking about her cooking.

Barbara and my uncle Jim ran a restaurant while I was in high school, and I worked there most evenings and weekends. She gave most of the staff Sundays off, so on those days she and I would run the restaurant together. Barbara was such a joy to work with, and whenever she had a chance to take a break from the front of the restaurant, she used to come back to the kitchen to help me prepare orders and wash dishes, then she would cook something special, just for us. After we closed she'd say, "Buddy boy [she called everyone 'buddy boy'], you want a plate?"

I don't think I could ever duplicate Aunt Barbara's gumbo, but I know this dish will make her proud. The chicken thighs in it are so flavorful, and andouille sausage is essential in any great New Orleans–style gumbo. Don't be intimidated about making the roux. The key is to stir constantly, so the oil and flour don't burn. You will know it's done when the color darkens. Serve the gumbo hot over long-grain rice—buddy boy, it's on! (Thanks, Aunt Barbara, for great food and lovely memories.)

½ cup plus 2 tablespoons vegetable oil, divided

½ cup all-purpose flour

1 large onion, chopped

1 green bell pepper, seeded and chopped

3 stalks celery, chopped

1 tablespoon Creole seasoning

¼ teaspoon cayenne pepper

1½ pounds andouille sausage, sliced into ¼-inch coins

3 pounds skinless, boneless chicken thighs

Kosher salt and freshly ground black pepper

8 cups homemade or low-sodium store-bought chicken broth

2 dried bay leaves

4 green onions, sliced

Dash of hot sauce

Dash of Worcestershire sauce

1 teaspoon filé powder (see Tip)

Hot cooked long-grain rice

---

continued on next page

continued from previous page

Heat ½ cup oil and the flour in a large heavy-bottomed skillet over medium heat, and cook, stirring constantly, for 15 minutes, until the roux changes to milk-chocolate color. Add the onion, bell pepper, and celery, and cook, stirring, until the vegetables are softened, about 10 minutes. For the last minute of cooking, sprinkle in the Creole seasoning and the cayenne. Remove from heat and reserve.

Add 2 tablespoons oil to coat the bottom of a large Dutch oven thinly, and heat over medium-high heat. Toss in the sausage, and cook, stirring, until browned and crisp around the edges, 6 to 8 minutes. Remove to a plate. Season the chicken thighs on both sides with salt and pepper, and brown, in two batches, 4 to 5 minutes per side. Remove to a plate. Stir the chicken broth into the Dutch oven, scraping up any browned bits on the bottom of the pan. Stir in the roux and the vegetables, the sausage, chicken, and bay leaves, and bring to a boil; reduce the heat to a simmer, and cook, uncovered, for 2 hours, stirring on occasion. Add the green onions, hot sauce, Worcestershire sauce, and filé powder. Taste for seasonings, and adjust as necessary. Remove the bay leaves, and serve the gumbo over some hot long-grain rice.

Serves 6 to 8

Tip Filé powder is made from the ground leaves of the sassafras tree. It's used to season and thicken gumbos and stews and can be found in good grocery stores.

Veggie Tortilla Soup

Gina We froze *everything* in my house when I was growing up. My mom used to make purposefully large batches of everything she cooked, so she could serve some for dinner and freeze the other portions. When we didn't have anything planned for dinner, we went straight to the freezer. Her veggie soup was always one of our favorites. This recipe is great because it's easy to make and packed with flavor. The chili powder is strong (like my man); the fire-roasted tomatoes add a smoky spice. Add some tortilla chips, sour cream, and cheese, and serve. Just be sure to make extra for frozen leftovers!

2 tablespoons olive oil

1 red onion, finely chopped

1 green bell pepper, seeded and finely chopped

3 cloves garlic, finely chopped

2 teaspoons chili powder

3½ cups homemade or low-sodium store-bought vegetable stock or chicken broth

Two 15-ounce cans black beans, drained and rinsed

One 14.5-ounce can fire-roasted diced tomatoes

2 ears corn (to yield 1½ cups kernels)

Kosher salt and freshly ground black pepper

1 cup slightly crushed tortilla chips

⅓ cup roughly chopped fresh cilantro

Shredded sharp cheddar and sour cream, for serving (optional)

Heat the oil in a large heavy-bottomed pot over medium-high heat. Sauté the onion and bell pepper until softened, about 4 minutes. Stir in the garlic and chili powder, and cook for 1 more minute, until fragrant. Pour in the stock, black beans, tomatoes, and corn, and bring to a boil. Reduce heat, and simmer for 15 minutes. Season with salt and pepper.

Stir in the tortilla chips and cilantro, and serve, if desired, topped with shredded cheese and sour cream.

Serves 4 to 6

Corn and Crab Chowder

Gina Spenser and Shelbi have been fans of crab since they were little girls, which strikes me as funny when I think about what I liked to eat when I was a child (hint: PB&J). This soup, with the sweet corn and Vidalia onion balancing out the crab and spices, is one of their favorite dishes. It is hearty enough to be served on its own, but I also like it with a fresh salad.

---

5 ears corn (to yield about 4½ cups
    corn kernels)
4 tablespoons unsalted butter
1 Vidalia onion, chopped
2 stalks celery, chopped
3 cloves garlic, chopped
⅓ cup all-purpose flour
4 cups homemade or low-sodium
    store-bought chicken broth
3 Yukon Gold potatoes (1½ pounds),
    scrubbed and cubed

1 dried bay leaf
2 cups whole milk
One 8-ounce can crabmeat
    (claw or lump)
1 teaspoon chopped fresh thyme
Kosher salt and freshly ground
    black pepper
Dash of hot sauce
Dash of Worcestershire
    sauce

Cut the corn kernels from the cobs and put them in a bowl. Use your knife to scrape the cobs to release the milky liquid. Reserve.

Melt the butter in a large saucepan or soup pot over medium heat. Once it's foamy and melted, add the onion, celery, and garlic, and sauté until softened, about 5 minutes. Sprinkle in the flour, and stir until thoroughly combined with the vegetables, about 2 minutes. Pour in the chicken broth, and toss in the potatoes and bay leaf and simmer for 10 to 12 minutes, or until the potatoes are soft. Stir in the milk, crab, corn and its liquid, and thyme, and simmer for an additional 10 minutes. Adjust seasoning with salt, lots of black pepper, hot sauce, and Worcestershire sauce. Remove the bay leaf before serving.

Serves 6 to 8

Brunswick Stew

Pat   Brunswick stew is a Southern recipe that's been around for over 100 years. It's a true everything-but-the-kitchen-sink dish, and the recipe generally works with whatever you have in your fridge. Most of the time, I didn't know what was actually in my grandmother's stew, nor did I care. All I knew was that it was damn good.

There are two meats that are always plentiful in our house: chicken and smoked pulled pork. I was in my freezer just the other day and saw a bag of cooked leftover meat. I looked a little closer and, sure enough, it was a bag of smoked pulled pork. Into the pot it went, along with the rest of the ingredients in this recipe.

---

2 tablespoons vegetable oil
1 large Vidalia onion, chopped
3 cups homemade or low-sodium
   store-bought chicken broth
¾ cup BBQ Sauce (page 99)
One 14.5-ounce can diced tomatoes
One 14.5-ounce can creamed corn

1 tablespoon yellow mustard
One 16-ounce package frozen
   baby lima beans, thawed
1½ pounds smoked pulled pork
¾ pound cooked chicken, chopped
Kosher salt and freshly ground
   black pepper

Heat the oil in a large Dutch oven or heavy-bottomed soup pot over medium-high heat. Add the onion, and sauté until tender, about 4 minutes. Add the chicken broth, barbecue sauce, diced tomatoes, creamed corn, and mustard. Bring to a boil, then reduce to a low simmer; cook, uncovered, stirring occasionally, for 2 hours.

Stir in the lima beans, pork, and chicken, and simmer for 8 more minutes. Taste, and adjust seasoning as necessary.

Serves 8

Lemony Chicken and Kale Soup

Gina For the longest time, I thought kale was used exclusively as decoration for party trays. Once I tried it, it was love at first bite, and kale has been a staple in my grocery basket ever since. It's a denser green that, along with the chicken, makes this soup hearty enough to be served as a meal.

2 tablespoons olive oil
1 medium onion, finely chopped
3 cloves garlic, finely chopped
2 bone-in, skin-on chicken-breast halves
    (about 2 pounds)
6 cups homemade or low-sodium
    store-bought chicken broth

Juice of 2 lemons
1 small bunch kale (8 ounces),
    stems removed, finely chopped
1 cup orzo
Kosher salt and freshly ground
    black pepper

Heat the oil in a large Dutch oven over medium-high heat. Stir in the onion, and sauté until tender, about 4 minutes. Toss in the garlic, and sauté until fragrant, about 1 minute more. Add both chicken pieces, and cover with broth. Bring broth up to a boil, reduce to a simmer, and cover with a tight-fitting lid. Cook the chicken for 15 minutes, or until it's cooked through.

Using tongs, remove the chicken to a plate until cool enough to handle. Shred the chicken with a fork, and then chop into bite-sized pieces.

Squeeze in the lemon juice, and slip the kale and the orzo into the pot. Cook for 8 minutes, or until orzo is tender and kale is soft. Stir in the chicken, taste for seasoning, and adjust as necessary.

Serves 6

Sweets

Peach and Almond Crisp

Mama Daisy's Chocolate-Frosted Cake

Lemon Meringue Pie

Fried Apple Hand Pies

Sour Cream Bundt Cake

Summer Fruit Cobbler

Homemade Peach Ice Cream

Banana Pudding Ice Cream

Blackberry Frozen Yogurt

Pat Both our grandparents grew peach trees in their backyards, and Gina and I spent plenty of summer afternoons when we were younger climbing them and pulling the juicy peaches right off the branches. That's right—Gina used to climb trees! Those peaches inspired many of the recipes in this chapter, including a delicious Peach and Almond Crisp and Homemade Peach Ice Cream. The Sour Cream Bundt Cake is an updated version of Gina's mom's pound cake, and by far the easiest and prettiest cake to display on your counter. We like to end our dinners with a little something sweet, and this chapter has something for everyone.

Peach and Almond Crisp

Gina Summer desserts in Memphis are always really special when peaches are involved. If my mom needed peaches for a recipe when we were kids, she'd send me out to the backyard to pull some off the trees behind our house. It was the one fruit we never had to buy at the market.

Peaches are sweet enough on their own, but we added a little brown sugar to the filling in the recipe as a cooking agent. As the brown sugar dissolves, the filling will become syrupy and thick. The topping is a combination of nutty almonds and crispy oats. The key to the topping is to make sure your butter is cold; it's what holds everything together. I like to serve my crisps hot, straight from the oven, with a big scoop of vanilla ice cream on top. One bite of this and you just might plant your own backyard peach trees.

FILLING

6 ripe peaches (2½ pounds), pitted and
   sliced into ½-inch wedges
⅓ cup light-brown sugar
Juice of 1 lemon
2 tablespoons all-purpose flour
2 tablespoons unsalted butter,
   sliced into small pats, plus butter
   for dish

TOPPING

¾ cup all-purpose flour
½ cup rolled oats
½ cup granulated white sugar
¼ cup packed brown sugar
8 tablespoons unsalted butter, cold, cut
   into ½-inch cubes
½ cup sliced almonds, roughly chopped
Vanilla ice cream (optional)

Preheat oven to 375 degrees F. Butter a 1½-quart casserole dish.

Make the filling: Toss the peaches, brown sugar, and lemon juice in a medium bowl, and let sit out for 10 minutes. Mix in the flour, add to the casserole dish, and dot with the pats of butter.

Make the topping: In a bowl, whisk together the flour, oats, and both sugars. Mix in the butter with your fingers, and blend until the flour resembles pea-sized lumps. Add the almonds, and toss well. Grab a small handful of topping, squeeze together to make large chunks, and spread evenly over the top of the peaches. Bake the crisp for 30 minutes, until bubbling and golden on top. Top with vanilla ice cream, if desired.

Serves 6 to 8

Mama Daisy's Chocolate-Frosted Cake

Pat This yellow cake with chocolate icing has to be the most delicious dessert Mama Daisy used to make. Whenever I visited her, I'd run straight to the kitchen and raise the lid of her cake plate with the hope of finding a freshly baked piece of chocolate-frosted cake. Not only is this cake delicious; it couldn't be simpler to make. It's based on an old-fashioned 1-2-3-4 yellow cake recipe. These always contain 1 cup of butter, 2 cups of sugar, 3 cups of flour, and 4 eggs. The cake is light and airy, and the rich, creamy frosting is a perfect contrast.

We tried to duplicate Mama Daisy's Southern style, and the only difference is that our cake is three layers instead of four. Even though her cake had four layers, Mama Daisy only used two cake pans. She would remove each cake and slice it with a sharp knife to divide it into two cakes. Amazingly, every piece was evenly sliced. Not even my mom could match her steady hand on this cake, which is why we made it easier and divided the batter between three pans. The icing is applied between the layers, which helps keep the cake from falling and makes each bite heavenly. Mama Daisy would be proud to know that Gina and I have tried our darnedest to keep her Southern tradition alive.

Nonstick spray

3 cups all-purpose flour, plus more for dusting

1 cup (2 sticks) unsalted butter, at room temperature

2 cups sugar

1 tablespoon baking powder

1 teaspoon baking soda

¾ teaspoon kosher salt

4 eggs

2 teaspoons pure vanilla extract

1 cup whole milk

Chocolate Frosting (recipe follows)

Preheat oven to 350 degrees F, and adjust racks to the center of the oven. Spray three 9-inch round cake pans lightly with nonstick spray. Dust the pans lightly with flour.

Put the butter in the bowl of a stand mixer, and beat until creamy, about 1 minute. Add the sugar, and beat until light and fluffy, about 7 minutes.

Meanwhile, put the flour, baking powder, baking soda, and salt in a medium bowl, and whisk together until well blended.

Add the eggs to the butter and sugar, one at a time. Stir the vanilla extract into the milk, and alternately beat into the butter mixture the flour mixture and the milk, beginning and ending with the flour, until evenly blended and smooth, scraping down the sides with a rubber spatula. Divide the batter into the prepared pans.

Bake the cakes for 30 minutes, or until a toothpick inserted into the center of each cake

continued on next page

continued from previous page

comes out clean. Cool for 10 minutes in the pans before inverting onto a cooling rack. Let cool completely before frosting.

To assemble the cake: Place one layer, top side down, on a cake stand. Spread a thick layer of frosting across the top, all the way to the edges. Place the next layer right on top, and add another layer of frosting. Top with the final layer, dome side up for the nice old-fashioned look, and frost the top and sides of the cake by working from the center of the cake toward the edges.

Chocolate Frosting

4 cups confectioners' sugar
   (1-pound bag)
¾ cup unsweetened cocoa powder
⅛ teaspoon kosher salt

2 sticks (1 cup) unsalted butter,
   at room temperature
2 teaspoons pure vanilla extract
½ cup whole milk

Put the confectioners' sugar, cocoa powder, and salt in a medium bowl, and whisk until smooth and blended.

Put the butter in the bowl of a stand mixer, and beat until creamy. Add the cocoa mixture by scoopfuls, beating until well combined. Beat in the vanilla, then add the milk until it reaches a smooth and creamy, spreadable consistency.

Serves 12

Lemon Meringue Pie

Pat After dinner, if we ate everything on our plates, my mom or grandmother would always ask, "Do you want something sweet?" Those old-school women would do whatever it took to get you to eat everything on your plate; that included bribes.

I would eat just about anything for this lemon-meringue pie—it's that good. Instead of graham crackers, we use Biscoff cookies for our crust, and it is really simple: melted butter, sugar, and cookie crumbs. The next step is the filling, and then it's meringue time, which is usually when I shout for Gina if she's not in the kitchen with me. Making the meringue is similar to making whipped cream. Gina always shows patience with her hand mixer and wants the swirls to be perfect. She says I'm too messy when it comes to adding our topping. I'd be more upset about that, but her meringue is too good for me to stay mad.

CRUST

2 cups finely ground cookie crumbs made from Biscoff cookies

¼ cup sugar

7 tablespoons unsalted butter, melted

FILLING

1½ cups sugar

¼ cup cornstarch

⅛ teaspoon kosher salt

½ cup lemon juice (from 3 large lemons)

4 large eggs, plus 1 yolk

1 teaspoon pure vanilla extract

½ teaspoon grated lemon zest

2 tablespoons unsalted butter, sliced

MERINGUE

4 large egg whites, at room temperature

¼ teaspoon cream of tartar

⅛ teaspoon kosher salt

1 teaspoon pure vanilla extract

⅓ cup sugar

Make the crust: Combine the cookie crumbs, sugar, and melted butter in a medium bowl. Put in a 9-inch pie plate, and press along the sides and bottom to coat evenly. Bake for 10 minutes. Let cool completely.

Make the filling: In a medium saucepan, whisk the sugar, cornstarch, and salt together until well blended. Stir in the lemon juice and eggs and yolk. Turn heat to medium, and continue to whisk as the mixture comes up to a simmer. Cook and whisk for about 4 minutes, until filling is thick and glossy. Remove from the heat, and whisk in the vanilla extract, lemon zest, and butter. Pour into the prepared crust. Use your rubber spatula to spread out the filling and smooth the top.

continued on next page

continued from previous page

Preheat oven to 350 degrees F.

Make the meringue: Using a stand mixer fitted with the whisk attachment, beat the egg whites, cream of tartar, salt, and vanilla extract until foamy. Slowly and very gradually add the sugar while the machine is running, and continue beating until meringue is stiff and glossy, about 4 minutes.

Spread the meringue over the filling, and swirl to cover entire top of the pie, making sure it's touching the crust. Bake for 15 minutes, until lightly golden. Allow to cool for 1 hour before serving.

Serves 6 to 8

MAMA DAISY BAKING

Pat Mama Daisy had just about the largest wooden rolling pin I have ever seen. I can still see her wielding that big, heavy thing with such expertise, a far cry from today's typical plastic pins! But I'd say one of her most prized and important baking instruments was a massive (to me, anyway) mixer with a thick black cord attached. Once she turned it on, it was so loud and powerful that it shook the entire kitchen!

Fried Apple Hand Pies

Gina My great-grandmother Mama Callie took just as much pride in preparing her desserts as she did the main course. She liked to bake with apples and was famous for her apple pies. Even the way she peeled apples was impressive. She used to take a knife and peel an entire Granny Smith without ever breaking the peel. I mean, this woman had skills!

As good as the apple filling is, I fell in love with her fried apple hand pies because of the crust. In these mini–apple pies, a drop of filling is completely surrounded by a shell of crispy crust. Mama Callie made everything by hand, but we've made the recipe easier by using a food processor to make the crust. You can add little lines around the edges with the tip of a fork. Then it's off to fry in some fresh hot peanut oil. Dust a little cinnamon sugar on top while they are still hot. I'm sure Mama Callie would be proud.

CRUST

2 cups all-purpose flour, plus more for
   work surface

1 tablespoon granulated white sugar

½ teaspoon kosher salt

½ cup (1 stick) unsalted butter, cubed
   and chilled

2 tablespoons vegetable shortening,
   chilled

¼ cup ice-cold water

FILLING

3 tablespoons unsalted butter

1 medium Granny Smith apple, peeled
   and diced

1 medium Golden Delicious apple, peeled
   and diced

¼ cup light-brown sugar

1½ teaspoons ground cinnamon

⅛ teaspoon freshly grated nutmeg

⅛ teaspoon ground ginger

Pinch of kosher salt

Peanut oil, for frying

Cinnamon Sugar, for dusting
   (recipe follows)

Make the crust: Blend together the flour, sugar, and salt in a food processor. Add the cold butter and shortening, and pulse just a few times, until the mixture looks like coarse meal. Add the cold water, and process until the dough looks crumbly. Check the dough by squeezing it between your fingers; it should clump together.

Transfer the dough to a floured work surface, and knead gently a few times, until it comes together. Divide in two, and wrap the dough in plastic wrap, then refrigerate for at least 1 hour. Remove the dough from the refrigerator, and let sit out for 10 minutes to soften slightly before rolling out.

continued on page 181

continued from page 179

Make the filling: Melt the butter in a large sauté pan over medium-high heat. Once it's foamy, add the apples, and sauté until soft, about 4 minutes. Reduce heat to medium, and stir in the brown sugar, cinnamon, nutmeg, ginger, and salt. Cook, stirring, for another 5 to 6 minutes, until the apples are very soft but still hold their shape. Remove from the pan, and cool completely.

On a lightly floured work surface, working one disc at a time, roll out each dough ball to about ¼-inch thickness. Use a 4½-inch biscuit cutter to cut out circles. Top each round with a heaping tablespoon of filling. Fold the circles in half, lightly wet the edges with water, and seal with tines of a fork. Gather dough scraps, knead together gently into a new disc, and refrigerate for 10 minutes. Roll out the scraps, cut more rounds, and repeat. Place on a sheet tray, and refrigerate again until chilled, about 20 minutes.

Heat 1½ inches of oil in a heavy skillet over medium-high heat. Using a candy thermometer, heat to 350 degrees F. Fry the pies in batches until golden and crisp, about 3 minutes total, flipping about halfway through, so they cook evenly. Transfer to a paper-towel-lined sheet tray to drain. Allow to cool slightly, and then roll in a plate of cinnamon sugar. These are best served warm.

Makes 10 pies

Tip Since the dough needs to be chilled, you can always make it the day before.

Cinnamon Sugar

¼ cup sugar	¼ teaspoon ground cinnamon

Whisk ingredients together until combined.

Makes about ¼ cup

Sour Cream Bundt Cake

Pat   Every mother and grandmother I knew when I was growing up had a secret pound-cake recipe. My favorite was my aunt's homemade pound cake topped with fresh strawberries and one scoop of vanilla ice cream. Gina's mom is the pound-cake queen of the family these days, and she brings her signature pound cake over to our house for every family gathering. She inherited her recipe from her grandmother, and has since passed it on to me and Gina. This Bundt is a version of that original recipe. It looks beautiful displayed on a platter and the cake is so moist from the sour cream, there's no need for icing. Just a little powdered sugar on top to sweeten it up, and you're set!

Nonstick spray
3 cups all-purpose flour, plus more
   for dusting the pan
1 cup (2 sticks) unsalted butter,
   at room temperature
3 cups granulated sugar
¾ teaspoon kosher salt

½ teaspoon baking powder
¼ teaspoon baking soda
6 large eggs, at room temperature
1 cup sour cream, at room temperature
1½ teaspoons pure vanilla extract
¾ teaspoon almond extract
Confectioners' sugar, for dusting

Preheat oven to 350 degrees F. Spray a Bundt pan with nonstick spray, and lightly dust with flour, shaking out excess.

In the large bowl of a stand mixer fitted with the paddle attachment, beat the butter and granulated sugar together until light and fluffy, about 5 minutes.

While the butter and sugar are creaming, whisk together the flour, salt, baking powder, and baking soda in a medium bowl. Reserve.

Add the eggs to the mixer while it's running, one a time, beating well after each addition. Beat in the sour cream, and then the extracts. Add the dry ingredients in increments. Mix until combined.

Pour batter into the prepared Bundt pan. Bake for 1 hour and 10 minutes, or until a toothpick inserted into the center comes out clean. Let cool on a wire rack before turning out. Dust top with confectioners' sugar.

Serves 10

Summer Fruit Cobbler

Gina Restaurants in the South serve peach cobbler like sweet tea—lots of it, all the time. I wanted to create a cobbler that incorporated all the flavors of summer, and this recipe has a little bit of everything in it. The first time I prepared this for Pat and the girls, I asked Pat what fruits he thought were in there, and his reply was "I don't care, it's so damn good, it really doesn't matter at this point."

FILLING

5 peaches (2 pounds), pitted, peeled, and cut into ½-inch slices (for peeling, see next recipe Tip)

2 plums (¾ pound), pitted and cut into ½-inch slices

2 nectarines (¾ pound), pitted and cut into ½-inch slices

1 cup sugar

½ cup water

1 teaspoon pure vanilla extract

Pinch of kosher salt

CRUST

1 cup self-rising flour

1 cup sugar

¼ teaspoon ground cinnamon

¼ teaspoon kosher salt

¼ cup whole milk

1 egg, beaten

1 tablespoon unsalted butter, melted

Preheat oven to 350 degrees F.

Make the filling: Toss the peaches, plums, nectarines, sugar, water, vanilla extract, and salt together in a large saucepan or skillet over medium-high heat. Bring to a simmer, and cook for 10 minutes, stirring occasionally. Put in a 2-quart square casserole dish.

Make the crust: In a medium bowl, combine the self-rising flour, sugar, cinnamon, salt, milk, egg, and butter. Top the fruit filling with the batter in spoonfuls. Place on a sheet tray, and bake for 35 to 40 minutes, until topping is golden and puffy.

Serves 6 to 8

Homemade Peach Ice Cream

Pat I would never have dreamed that making ice cream could be so easy. I watched my grandma Rena make it when I was younger, and it seemed like such hard work. She would use a hand-cranked ice-cream maker made out of a wooden barrel and rock salt. The whole process took so long I'd always run out of the kitchen to play outside while she worked. She had a backyard full of peach trees, and my brothers and I used to climb them and eat the peaches right off the branches—dirt and all. I was technically working, too, since my job was to collect peaches for her to cook with. This ice cream is a tribute to her, and, with modern ice-cream makers, a little easier to make. One bite and I feel like I'm back in the peach trees behind Mama Rena's house.

---

2 ripe peaches, peeled and chopped
  (see Tip)
¼ cup peach nectar
One 14-ounce can sweetened condensed
  milk

2 cups heavy cream
1 teaspoon pure vanilla extract
Pinch of kosher salt

A full 24 hours before you make your ice cream, place your ice-cream insert in the freezer.

Put the chopped peaches in a bowl along with peach nectar. Toss well, and cover. Let the peaches sit at room temperature for 30 minutes.

Purée the peaches in a food processor. Transfer the mixture to a bowl, and mix in the sweetened condensed milk, heavy cream, vanilla extract, and salt. Cover with plastic wrap and place in the refrigerator to chill for 1 hour.

Turn on your ice-cream machine, and pour the peach mixture into the chilled insert. Churn until the mixture looks like soft-serve, about 15 minutes. Enjoy soft, or place in a covered container and freeze for several hours until hard.

Serves 6

Tip To peel peaches, make an "X" on the bottom of the peach with a paring knife, place in a pot of boiling water, making sure it's completely covered, and blanch for 20 seconds or up to 1 minute (depending on ripeness). Plunge into a bowl of ice water to stop the cooking, and then peel the fuzzy skin right off.

Banana Pudding Ice Cream

Pat Banana pudding was always a hit-or-miss dessert for me: I either loved it or I didn't. Some people used to serve it cold, and others, like my mom, actually baked it and turned it into a warm dessert. In our frozen version, there's never a chance for the bananas to brown, and the wafers don't go soft. It's a dessert I love every time.

---

3 cups half-and-half

One 14-ounce can sweetened condensed milk

One 5.1-ounce package Banana Cream Instant Pudding

2 teaspoons pure vanilla extract

Pinch of kosher salt

1¼ cups crushed vanilla wafers

Sliced bananas, for serving

Homemade whipped cream, for serving

A full 24 hours before you make your ice cream, place your ice-cream insert in the freezer.

In a medium bowl, whisk together the half-and-half, sweetened condensed milk, pudding mix, vanilla extract, and salt. Cover with plastic wrap and place in the refrigerator to chill for 1 hour.

Turn on your ice-cream machine, and pour the mixture into the chilled insert. Churn until the mixture looks like soft-serve, about 15 minutes. Sprinkle in the vanilla wafers while it's running, and churn for 5 more minutes so the cookie crumbs are dispersed. Enjoy soft, or place in a covered container and freeze for several hours until hard. To serve, top with sliced bananas and homemade whipped cream.

Serves 8

HAND-CRANK ICE-CREAM MAKERS

Pat Mama Rena had a classic hand-crank ice-cream maker. It was made out of a wooden barrel with a manual handle to churn the cream. The area surrounding the container in the barrel was filled with ice and rock salt. I never understood that step as a kid. Turns out, the salt speeds up the cooling process and lowers the temperature enough to freeze the heavy cream. In the process of melting, the ice pulls the heat from the cream mixture. The addition of salt lowers the temperature of the ice to 27 degrees F (as opposed to 32) and makes the ice melt faster, causing the cream to become colder more quickly and preventing icy granules from forming.

Blackberry Frozen Yogurt

Pat   When I stayed at Mama Daisy's house during the summer months, she'd keep her windows up so that the fresh summer breeze could flow through her home. And when her blackberry cobbler was finished baking, she'd set it near the tiny window in her kitchen to cool. It wasn't long before everyone in the neighborhood knew what was for dessert—and came running. She made one fantastic blackberry cobbler. I always preferred ice cream, though, so I've adapted Mama Daisy's famous cobbler into a frozen yogurt that's just as good. The recipe follows the same process as our Homemade Peach Ice Cream (page 186), but replaces the heavy cream and condensed milk with tangy Greek yogurt, which goes better with the fresh blackberries.

One 12-ounce bag frozen blackberries, thawed but still cold

²/₃ cup superfine sugar

2 teaspoons pure vanilla extract

2 cups plain reduced-fat Greek yogurt, chilled

2 cups plain reduced-fat regular yogurt, chilled

A full 24 hours before you make your frozen yogurt, place your ice-cream insert in the freezer.

Put the berries, sugar, and vanilla extract in a large bowl, and mash gently with a wooden spoon. You want the berries to be broken up, but you still want a little texture. Let the berries sit out at room temperature for 5 minutes, stirring on occasion, until the sugar dissolves.

Add the yogurts to the berries, and mix well. Cover with plastic wrap and place in the refrigerator to chill for 15 minutes.

Turn on your ice-cream machine, and pour the yogurt mixture into the chilled insert. Churn until the mixture looks like soft-serve, 12 to 15 minutes. Enjoy soft, or place in a covered container and freeze for several hours, until scoopable.

Serves 6

Gina's Southern Cocktails

Gina's Green Tomato Sangria

Tupelo Sour

Memphis Mojito

Southern Jug Margarita

Planter's Punch

Blackberry Limeade

Gina You will find that most of these colorful cocktails are served in Southern jugs—a shout-out to Memphis and Southern hospitality. A traditional Southern jug was a narrow-necked glass or earthenware bottle with a cork top and a loop handle. (They always make me think of moonshine!) In this case, though, I'm talking about my family's definition of a Southern jug, which is the name we had for Mason jars. We always made large batches of our cocktails when we entertained, because someone was always asking, "What do you have to wet my whistle with?" We poured cocktails from large pitchers into Mason jars, and the cocktails always seemed to liven up the party.

Gina's Green Tomato Sangria

Gina   Sangria is a light and refreshing summer cocktail. The combination of fruits in this drink—peaches, lychees, green tomato, tomatillos, Granny Smith apple, and orange—gives this drink a crisp flavor. My favorite wine, Pinot Grigio, offsets the sweetness of the fruit and nectar. Poured over ice, this is the perfect summer cocktail.

One 750ml bottle dry white wine, such as Pinot Grigio

One 15-ounce can peaches in heavy syrup

15 ounces canned lychees in heavy syrup, chopped

2½ cups peach nectar

1 cup peach schnapps

1 green tomato, finely chopped

2 tomatillos, husks removed, finely chopped

1 Granny Smith apple, finely chopped

Juice of 1 lemon, plus 1 lemon, sliced

1 orange, sliced

½ cup loosely packed basil leaves, torn

Combine all the ingredients except basil, including the syrups for the fruit, in a gallon container, cover, and refrigerate for 24 hours. Add torn basil leaves right before serving. Serve in ice-filled Southern jugs (Mason jars).

Serves a crowd (Ten 12-ounce Mason jars)

Tip   This cocktail will keep for 5 days refrigerated.

Tupelo Sour

Gina My things-didn't-go-my-way-today drink always involves Jack Daniel's, but it's not something Southern ladies order at the bar without getting a few stares. The Tupelo Sour is my ladylike Jack Daniel's drink. It's heavy, tangy, and sweet, and oh so good.

2 ounces Jack Daniel's Tennessee Honey
1 heaping tablespoon orange
   marmalade

3 ounces lemonade
Orange zest, for garnish

Fill a cocktail shaker with ice. Add the Jack honey, orange marmalade, and lemonade, and shake for 20 seconds. Strain into an ice-filled rocks glass, and put some orange zest on top to garnish.

Makes 1 potent drink

Memphis Mojito

Gina Things are pretty relaxed in Memphis, and the mojito is definitely a cocktail for taking it easy. You can rim your glass with sugar, but only if you really feel like it. I always think it's best to let the bourbon speak loudest.

Sugar, for rimming glass (optional)
1½ teaspoons lime juice
1½ teaspoons simple syrup
  (see next recipe Tip)

5 to 7 fresh mint leaves
2 ounces Firefly bourbon
Club soda, for topping
Lime wedge, for garnish

If rimming your 12-ounce Southern jug (Mason jar) with sugar, dip the rim of your jar into water, then dip into sugar.

Put lime juice, simple syrup, and mint leaves in your jar, and muddle them well with a wooden spoon.

Fill the jar with ice, top with bourbon, and stir well to mix. Top the jar with club soda, add a lime wedge, and give it a stir again.

Makes 1 potent drink

Southern Jug Margarita

Gina We like to put a little flavor on everything in the South, and margaritas are not excluded from that. This cocktail is served best over ice, in a Southern jug, and on the porch during Memphis sunset. Or, well, wherever you are.

Kosher salt, for rimming glass
   (optional)
1½ ounces blanco tequila
1½ ounces orange-mango juice
1 ounce Cointreau

1 ounce lemon juice
1 ounce lime juice
1 ounce simple syrup
Lime wheel, for garnish

If rimming your 12-ounce Southern jug (Mason jar) with salt, dip the rim of your jar into water, then dip into salt.

Fill your jar with ice, and top with the tequila, orange-mango juice, Cointreau, lemon juice, lime juice, and simple syrup. Stir well, to combine and chill the ingredients. Serve garnished with a wheel of lime.

Makes 1 potent drink

Tip In case you don't remember, simple syrup is just 1 cup of water and 1 cup of sugar, stirred over heat until the sugar dissolves.

Planter's Punch

Gina This is the perfect cocktail for a party during the day. It's light, it's refreshing, but it packs a punch. And there's a fruit garnish in case you get hungry. If you're entertaining, triple the portions and make a jug, because one drink will not be enough to go around.

---

3 ounces dark rum

1½ ounces pineapple juice

1 ounce lemon juice

½ ounce grenadine

Dash of bitters

Orange slice and stemmed maraschino cherry, for garnish

Add the rum and the next four ingredients to an ice-filled cocktail shaker. Shake for 20 seconds, and strain into an ice-filled rocks glass. Garnish the drink with an orange slice and a cherry.

Punch Up Your Ice Cubes For a cute touch, add cherries to your ice tray and freeze them into cubes to add to your glasses.

Makes 1 drink

Blackberry Limeade

Gina My mom is a real Southern lady (she doesn't drink or smoke cigarettes). I gave her some sangria on a holiday once and she said, "This tastes like liquor." This beautiful cocktail is for my mom and all the other nondrinkers. Now, for the rest of us, add 2 ounces of vodka per glass, then top with limeade.

---

12 ounces fresh or frozen blackberries
   (thawed if frozen)
4½ cups chilled water, divided
1 cup freshly squeezed lime juice
   (from about 7 limes)

¾ cup superfine sugar
Lime slices and fresh blackberries,
   for garnish

Put the blackberries and ½ cup of the chilled water in a blender, and blend until smooth. Strain the blackberries through a fine-mesh sieve into a pitcher, and discard the seeds. Stir in remaining 4 cups water, lime juice, and superfine sugar. Stir until sugar is dissolved. Refrigerate until chilled, or serve immediately over ice. Garnish with lime slices and blackberries.

Serves 6 to 8

Acknowledgments

Pat Gina, once again, we have done it! Thank you for coauthoring this amazing book. We have shared some wonderful stories and delicious recipes. You are truly a fantastic partner and an incredible wife. Love you much!

Lorine Neely, my mom, thank you for helping me remember these wonderful stories from my childhood. The old stories of my time spent with Mama Daisy, Daddy Milton, Dye, and Mama Rena brought back so many cherished moments and helped me relive my childhood. Love you, and I promise to continue to pass these memories on to your grandchildren.

Gina I can't believe we are here again. . . . It is still amazing and unbelievable to me to have had a third opportunity to share family recipes that have touched our hearts for so long. Thank you to all of our supporters who have been there since day one. And I have to *thank* our girls for being so patient with sharing their parents—we know how you feel about it. Thanks to Pat for writing, sharing, and loving alongside with me. To my mom (Erma J. Ervin), my great-grandmother (Mama Callie), my sissies (Kim, Tanya, and Jackie) for spoiling/supporting me, and Nana (Alta Lemon), for providing the memories for these dishes and stories. This book would not be possible without my amazing *army* of supporters.

Mike Sword, you have been our rock! Your management skills and leadership continue to guide us in the right direction. We are blessed to have you on our team. To Janis Donnaud, Paul Bogaards, Elizabeth Lindsay, and the entire team at Knopf, together we have again created a collection of memorable dishes from our history.

Huge hugs and thanks to Ann Volkwein and Brianna Beaudry! Ladies, we couldn't have recaptured this history of our lives without your vision and direction.

None of this would be possible without YOU, the best fans in the world, for your continued loving support and consistent loyalty. We will always be grateful to you.

Love you *all* and many thanks!

Index

A

almonds
  kale salad with chopped almonds, feta, and champagne vinaigrette, 79
  peach and almond crisp, 173
appetizers, snacks, and small bites, 33–53
  crunchy fried okra, 45
  deep-fried pickles, 46
  easy brie-sy baked Brie with walnuts and fresh strawberry jam, 51
  fried shrimp with hot pepper jelly dipping sauce, 50
  Gina's favorite black-eyed pea hummus with pita chips, 35
  Gina's hot feta and pimiento cheese spread, 49
  homemade fish sticks with tartar sauce, 52–3
  homemade onion dip with Old Bay potato chips, 40–2
  Memphis caviar, 38
  mini–crab cakes with smoked tomato mayo, 36–7
  Pat's spicy hot cheese dip, 43
  pepper pig candy, 48
apple
  apple, bacon, and bourbon stuffed pork chops, 119
  fried apple hand pies, 179–81

B

bacon
  apple, bacon, and bourbon stuffed pork chops, 119
  grilled steak salad with bacon and blue cheese, 85
banana pudding ice cream, 187
BBQ'd slaw dog, 132

BBQ sauce, 99
beef
  brown sugar and soy-marinated flank steak, 128
  country-fried steak with black pepper and cream gravy, 91–2
  grilled steak salad with bacon and blue cheese, 85
  old school braised oxtails, 95–6
  sloppy roast beef po' boy with debris gravy, 142–3
  tangy, sweet and sour pot roast, 93–4
  WTF burger, 149
beverages, see Gina's Southern cocktails
biscuits, easy buttermilk and cream, 15
blackberry
  blackberry frozen yogurt, 189
  blackberry limeade, 200
black-eyed peas
  black-eyed pea cakes, 74
  Gina's favorite black-eyed pea hummus with pita chips, 35
blue cheese, grilled steak salad with bacon and, 85
bourbon
  apple, bacon, and bourbon stuffed pork chops, 119
  bourbon French toast, 26
breadboxes, 17
breads and biscuits, 15–18
  easy buttermilk and cream biscuits, 15
  green onion and cheddar quick bread, 17
  old-fashioned yeast rolls, 16
  skillet corn bread, 18
breakfast, 21–31
  bourbon French toast, 26
  breakfast pot pie, 29

  eggs and cheese grits, 23
  griddled and glazed ham and eggs, 30
  pecan flapjacks, 25
  sausage cream gravy and biscuits, 31
Brie, easy brie-sy baked, with walnuts and fresh strawberry jam, 51
broccoli
  broccoli slaw, 86
  roasted broccoli with cheddar cheese sauce, 60
Brunswick stew, 167
buttermilk
  easy buttermilk and cream biscuits, 15
  shake it up salad with basil buttermilk dressing, 78
butters
  cinnamon honey butter, 12
  herb butter, 12

C

cakes
  Mama Daisy's chocolate-frosted cake, 175–6
  sour cream Bundt cake, 182
canning method, 7
Carter, Daisy (Mama Daisy), 14–15, 178
Carter, Milton (Daddy Milton), 131
casseroles and stews
  Brunswick stew, 167
  chicken pot pie, 156–7
  old-fashioned elbow mac and cheese, 155
  remixed green bean casserole, 153
  three-cheese pasta bake with spinach, 159

cast-iron skillets, 18

catfish

blackened catfish with Creole rémoulade, 110

smoked catfish with lemon and dill, 127

cauliflower, mashed with cheddar and chives, 67

cheddar cheese

green onion and cheddar quick bread, 17

mashed cauliflower with cheddar and chives, 67

roasted broccoli with cheddar cheese sauce, 60

cheese

cheesy double stuffed potatoes, 75

easy brie-sy baked Brie with walnuts and fresh strawberry jam, 51

eggs and cheese grits, 23

Gina's hot feta and pimiento cheese spread, 49

grilled steak salad with bacon and blue cheese, 85

old-fashioned mac and cheese, 155

Pat's spicy hot cheese dip, 43

three-cheese pasta bake with spinach, 159

see also cheddar cheese

chicken

big pot of chicken and sausage gumbo, 161–2

chicken pot pie, 156–7

fried chicken sandwich, 144

hot honey peach chicken, 103

lemony chicken and kale soup, 168

skillet roasted chicken, 105

smoked and spicy chicken wings, 123

smoky chicken and rice skillet, 102

Sunday fried chicken with red hot maple glaze, 107–8

weekday not fried chicken, 106

chocolate

chocolate frosting, 176

Mama Daisy's chocolate-frosted cake, 175–6

cinnamon honey butter, 12

cinnamon sugar, 181

Clark, Mama Callie, 96

collards, Gina's quick confetti, 64

compound butters, 12

corn

butter boiled corn and red potatoes with Creole seasoning, 61

corn and crab chowder, 164

smoky grilled corn in the husk, 135

corn bread, skillet, 18

crab

corn and crab chowder, 164

mini–crab cakes with smoked tomato mayo, 36–7

D

deep-fried pickles, 46

desserts, 173–89

banana pudding ice cream, 187

blackberry frozen yogurt, 189

fried apple hand pies, 179–81

homemade peach ice cream, 186

lemon meringue pie, 177–8

Mama Daisy's chocolate-frosted cake, 175–6

peach and almond crisp, 173

sour cream Bundt cake, 182

summer fruit cobbler, 185

dips

Gina's hot feta and pimiento cheese spread, 49

homemade onion dip with Old Bay potato chips, 40–2

Pat's spicy hot cheese dip, 43

E

eggs

eggs and cheese grits, 23

griddled and glazed ham and eggs, 30

Ervin, Erma Jean (Gina's mom), 154

F

feta, Gina's hot feta and pimiento cheese spread, 49

fish

blackened catfish with Creole rémoulade, 110

grilled salmon with peach relish, 117

halibut with kale and mushrooms, 111

homemade fish sticks with tartar sauce, 52–3

smoked catfish with lemon and dill, 127

see also shellfish

fried apple hand pies, 179–81

G

gadgetless kitchens, 86

Gina's Southern cocktails, 193–200

blackberry limeade, 200

Gina's green tomato sangria, 193

Memphis mojito, 197

planter's punch, 199

Southern jug margarita, 198

Tupelo sour, 194

"Grease Was the Way," 108

green bean casserole, remixed, 153

green onion and cheddar quick bread, 17

greens, spicy tomato stewed, 73

green tomato sangria, Gina's, 193

griddled and glazed ham and eggs, 30

grilled, *see* smoked and grilled

grits

eggs and cheese grits, 23

smoked sausage shrimp and grits, 112

H

halibut with kale and mushrooms, 111

hand-crank ice-cream makers, 188

herb butter, 12

homemade onion dip with Old Bay potato chips, 40–2

homemade pita chips, 35

hot pepper jelly dipping sauce, 50

I

ice cream

banana pudding ice cream, 187

homemade peach ice cream, 186

ice-cream makers, hand-crank, 188

J

jams and preserves, 3–11

hot pepper jelly, 6

pickled okra, 11

pickled peppers, 9

small batch strawberry jam, 5

sweet pickled relish, 10

K

kale

halibut with kale and mushrooms, 111

kale salad with chopped almonds, feta, and champagne vinaigrette, 79

lemony chicken and kale soup, 168

L

lemon

lemon meringue pie, 177–8

lemony chicken and kale soup, 168

smoked catfish with lemon and dill, 127

Lemon, Alta (Nana), 135

limeade, blackberry, 200

M

mac and cheese, old-fashioned, 155

Mama Daisy's chocolate-frosted cake, 175–6

margarita, Southern jug, 198

meats, 89–112

apple, bacon, and bourbon stuffed pork chops, 119

BBQ'd slaw dog, 132

brown sugar and soy–marinated flank steak, 128

country fried steak with black pepper and cream gravy, 91–2

griddled and glazed ham and eggs, 30

grilled steak salad with bacon and blue cheese, 85

low and slow pulled pork, 97–9

old school braised oxtails, 95–6

oven-roasted ribs (a.k.a. apartment ribs), 100

sloppy roast beef po' boy with debris gravy, 142–3

smoked sausage shrimp and grits, 112

tangy, sweet and sour pot roast, 93–4

WTF burger, 149

Memphis caviar, 38

Memphis mojito, 197

mushroom

grilled Vidalia onion and portobello burgers with smoked mozzarella and

roasted red pepper spread, 146–7

halibut with kale and mushrooms, 111

N

Neely, Gina, 4, 22, 34, 152, 192

Neely, Lorine (Pat's mom), 68

Neely, Pat, 56, 90, 116, 138, 172

O

okra

crunchy fried okra, 45

pickled okra, 11

Old Bay potato chips, 42

onions

grilled Vidalia onion and portobello burgers with smoked mozzarella and roasted red pepper spread, 146–7

homemade onion dip with Old Bay potato chips, 40–2

oxtails, old school braised, 95–6

P

peaches

grilled salmon with peach relish, 117

homemade peach ice cream, 186

hot honey peach chicken, 103

peach and almond crisp, 173

pecan flapjacks, 25

pepper pig candy, 48

peppers

grilled sausage and pepper sandwich, 124

hot pepper jelly, 6

pickled peppers, 9

roasted red pepper spread, 147

picnic rice salad, 87

pies
  fried apple hand pies, 179–81
  lemon meringue pie, 177–8
pimiento cheese, Gina's hot
    feta and pimiento cheese
    spread, 49
pinto beans, stewed, 57
pita chips, homemade, 35
planter's punch, 199
pork
  apple, bacon, and bourbon
    stuffed pork chops, 119
  BBQ'd slaw dog, 132
  griddled and glazed ham and
    eggs, 30
  low and slow pulled pork,
    97–9
  oven-roasted ribs (aka
    apartment ribs), 100
potatoes
  butter boiled corn and red
    potatoes with Creole
    seasoning, 61
  cheesy double stuffed
    potatoes, 75
  Old Bay potato chips, 42
  roasted fingerling potatoes with
    fresh herbs, 70
pot pie
  breakfast pot pie, 29
  chicken pot pie, 156–7

R
red hot maple glaze, 108
relish
  grilled salmon with peach relish,
    117
  sweet pickled relish, 10
rémoulade sauce, 111
rice
  picnic rice salad, 87
  smoky chicken and rice skillet,
    102
roasted red pepper spread, 147
roasted winter root vegetables, 58

S
salads
  broccoli slaw, 86
  charred vegetable salad with
    grilled croutons, 69
  grilled steak salad with bacon
    and blue cheese, 85
  kale salad with chopped
    almonds, feta, and
    champagne vinaigrette, 79
  not your basic sweet potato
    salad, 81
  picnic rice salad, 87
  shake it up salad with basil
    buttermilk dressing, 78
  summer green bean and barley
    salad, 76
  vinegar slaw, 82
salmon, grilled, with peach relish,
    117
sandwiches, 139–49
  fried chicken sandwich, 144
  grilled sausage and pepper
    sandwich, 124
  grilled Vidalia onion and
    portobello burgers with
    smoked mozzarella and
    roasted red pepper spread,
    146–7
  Pat's turkey patty melt,
    139–40
  sloppy roast beef po' boy with
    debris gravy, 142–3
  WTF burger, 149
sangria, Gina's green tomato, 193
sausage
  big pot of chicken and sausage
    gumbo, 161–2
  grilled sausage and pepper
    sandwich, 124
  sausage cream gravy and
    biscuits, 31
  smoked sausage shrimp and
    grits, 112
shake it up salad with basil
    buttermilk dressing, 78

shellfish
  corn and crab chowder, 164
  fried shrimp with hot pepper
    jelly dipping sauce, 50
  mini–crab cakes with smoked
    tomato mayo, 36–7
  smoked sausage shrimp and
    grits, 112
  see also fish
shrimp
  fried shrimp with hot pepper
    jelly dipping sauce, 50
  smoked sausage shrimp and
    grits, 112
side dishes and veggies
  black-eyed pea cakes, 74
  butter boiled corn and red
    potatoes with Creole
    seasoning, 61
  cheesy double stuffed
    potatoes, 75
  easy grilled veggie platter with
    champagne vinaigrette, 133
  Gina's quick confetti collards, 64
  grilled succotash, 63
  mashed cauliflower with
    cheddar and chives, 67
  roasted broccoli with cheddar
    sauce, 60
  roasted fingerling potatoes with
    fresh herbs, 70
  roasted winter root
    vegetables, 58
  spicy tomato stewed greens, 73
  stewed pinto beans, 57
  see also salads
skillet dishes
  skillet corn bread, 18
  skillet roasted chicken, 105
  smoky chicken and rice skillet,
    102
skillets, cast-iron, 18
slaw
  BBQ'd slaw dog, 132
  broccoli slaw, 86
  vinegar slaw, 82

smoked and grilled, 115–35
  apple, bacon and bourbon
    stuffed pork chops, 119
  BBQ'd slaw dog, 132
  brown sugar and soy–marinated
    flank steak, 128
  charred vegetable salad with
    grilled croutons, 69
  easy grilled veggie platter with
    champagne vinaigrette,
    133
  grilled salmon with peach relish,
    117
  grilled sausage and pepper
    sandwich, 124
  grilled succotash, 63
  grilled turkey breast with
    mayonnaise marinade and
    mop sauce, 130
  smoked and spicy chicken
    wings, 123
  smoked catfish with lemon and
    dill, 127
  smoked tomato mayo, 37
  smoky grilled corn in the husk,
    135
smoking meats and vegetables,
  120–1

snacks, *see* appetizers, snacks, and
  small bites
soups
  big pot of chicken and sausage
    gumbo, 161–2
  corn and crab chowder, 164
  lemony chicken and kale soup,
    168
  tomato bisque, 160
  veggie tortilla soup, 163
sour cream Bundt cake, 182
Southern jug margarita, 198
strawberry jam, small batch, 5
succotash, grilled, 63
summer fruit cobbler, 185
summer green bean and barley
  salad, 76
sweet potato salad, not your
  basic, 81
sweets, *see* desserts

T

tartar sauce, 53
thousand island dressing, 140
tomato
  Gina's green tomato sangria,
    193

mini–crab cakes with smoked
  tomato mayo, 36–7
  smoked tomato mayo, 37
  spicy tomato stewed greens, 73
  tomato bisque, 160
Tupelo sour, 194
turkey
  grilled turkey breast with
    mayonnaise marinade and
    mop sauce, 130
  Pat's turkey patty melt,
    139–40

V

vegetables, *see* side dishes and
  veggies
veggie tortilla soup, 163
vinegar slaw, 82

W

Wright, Irene (Mama Rena), 47
Wright, Rufus (Dye), 126

Y

yeast rolls, old-fashioned, 16

A NOTE ABOUT THE AUTHORS

Pat and Gina Neely are restaurateurs, best-selling authors, popular speakers, and hosts of the Food Network hit series *Down Home with the Neelys*. They recently opened their first New York City restaurant, Neely's Barbecue Parlor. They live with their daughters in Memphis, where they enjoy cooking at home with family and friends.

Ann Volkwein is a best-selling food-and-lifestyle author based in New York City and Austin, Texas. Her previous books include *The Neelys' Celebration Cookbook*, *The Arthur Avenue Cookbook*, *Chinatown New York*, *Mixt Salads* (with Andrew Swallow), and, with Guy Fieri, *Diners, Drive-Ins, and Dives; More Diners, Drive-Ins, and Dives;* and *Guy Fieri Food*.

A NOTE ON THE TYPE

This book was set in Thesis, a typeface created by the Dutch designer Lucas de Groot (born 1963) and released in 1994 by the FontFabrik foundry in Berlin. Originally known as Parenthesis, the Thesis family of fonts is unusual in including a serif font, a sans serif font, and a "mixed" font, which all strive to harmonize the traditionally disparate styles. In spite of its idiosyncratic character mapping, Thesis attempts to provide a complete solution to text and display type design.

COMPOSED BY NORTH MARKET STREET GRAPHICS, LANCASTER, PENNSYLVANIA

PRINTED AND BOUND BY RR DONNELLEY, CRAWFORDSVILLE, INDIANA

DESIGNED BY MAGGIE HINDERS